Tea & Sweets

Tea & Sweets

Fabulous Desserts *for* Afternoon Tea

hm|books

hm|books

EDITOR *Lorna Reeves*
CREATIVE DIRECTOR/PHOTOGRAPHY *Mac Jamieson*
ART DIRECTOR *Cailyn Haynes*
ASSOCIATE EDITOR *Betty Terry*
COPY EDITOR *Nancy Ogburn*
EDITORIAL ASSISTANT *Kellie Grammer*
STYLIST *Lucy W. Herndon*
SENIOR PHOTOGRAPHER *John O'Hagan*
PHOTOGRAPHERS *Sarah Arrington, William Dickey, Kamin H. Williams*
TEST KITCHEN DIRECTOR *Janice Ritter*
TEST KITCHEN PROFESSIONAL *Janet Lambert*
SENIOR DIGITAL IMAGING SPECIALIST *Delisa McDaniel*
DIGITAL IMAGING SPECIALIST *Clark Densmore*

hm
hoffmanmedia

PRESIDENT *Phyllis Hoffman DePiano*
EXECUTIVE VICE PRESIDENT/COO *Eric W. Hoffman*
EXECUTIVE VICE PRESIDENT/CCO *Brian Hart Hoffman*
EXECUTIVE VICE PRESIDENT/CFO *G. Marc Neas*
VICE PRESIDENT/FINANCE *Michael Adams*
VICE PRESIDENT/MANUFACTURING *Greg Baugh*
VICE PRESIDENT/EDITORIAL *Cindy Smith Cooper*
VICE PRESIDENT/CONSUMER MARKETING *Silvia Rider*
VICE PRESIDENT/ADMINISTRATION *Lynn Lee Terry*

First published in 2014 by Hoffman Media, LLC
Birmingham, Alabama
With offices at
1900 International Park Drive, Suite 50
Birmingham, Alabama 35243
hoffmanmedia.com

ISBN 978-1-940772-10-3
Printed in Mexico

ON THE COVER: Brownie Tart (page 50), Blueberry-Lemon Mini Cheesecakes (page 63), White Chocolate–Lemon Cake (page 27), Macadamia–Vanilla Bean Macarons (page 84), Raspberry French Macarons (page 84), Matcha French Macarons (page 85). Recipe development and food styling by Janet Lambert
Photography by Kamin H. Williams
Photo styling by Lucy W. Herndon

STENCILED
GINGERBREAD COOKIES
(recipe on page 90)

Contents

Introduction

TEATIME CAN BE SUCH AN ENJOYABLE OCCASION—lovely table settings, a pot of well-prepared tea, and dainty, delicious food to accompany it all.

People may differ as to whether the scones course should be served before or after the tea sandwiches and other savories, but there's little discussion about the appropriate place of the sweets course—that is, unless you subscribe to the mantra "Life is short; eat dessert first!"

Traditionally, sweets are served as the last course of a proper afternoon tea and should be displayed on the top plate of a tiered stand. If the size of the party or the treats warrants, an entire tiered server may be devoted to this course and even used as a tempting centerpiece. Large cakes are always pretty whole or cut into individual servings and artfully arranged on pedestal platters—and attractively garnished. Whatever the approach, this collection of recipes, some of which are gluten-free, will satisfy virtually any sweet tooth. Most of the recipes were developed in *TeaTime*'s test kitchen exclusively for this book, while others were contributed by select tearooms or have appeared in the pages of the magazine. Regardless of the source, the cakes and cupcakes, tarts and cheesecakes, and cookies and bars, as well as an assortment of other desserts presented here, will be perfect for the many occasions for tea, be it a simple snack for a few or an elegant event for a crowd.

The savvy host will ensure the right tea accompanies the foods on the teatime menu. Our pairing guidelines (page 11) and tea-steeping basics (page 10) will prove most helpful in selecting and preparing a delightful infusion best suited to the flavors of the sweets.

When you place any of these desserts before your guests, they will surely be convinced that, indeed, you saved the best for last.

Tea-Steeping Guide

The quality of the tea served at a tea party is as important as the food and the décor. To be sure your infusion is successful every time, here are some basic guidelines to follow.

WATER

Always use the best water possible. If the water tastes good, so will your tea. Heat the water on the stove top or in an electric kettle to the desired temperature. A microwave oven is not recommended.

TEMPERATURE

Heating the water to the correct temperature is arguably one of the most important factors in making a great pot of tea. Pouring boiling water on green, white, or oolong tea leaves can result in a very unpleasant brew. Always refer to the tea purveyor's packaging for specific instructions, but in general, use 170° to 195° water for these delicate tea types. Reserve boiling (212°) water for black and puerh teas, as well as herbal and fruit tisanes.

TEAPOT

If the teapot you plan to use is delicate, warm it with hot tap water first to avert possible cracking. Discard this water before adding the tea leaves or tea bags.

TEA

Use the highest-quality tea you can afford, whether loose leaf or prepackaged in bags or sachets. Remember that these better teas can often be steeped more than once. When using loose-leaf tea, generally use 1 generous teaspoon of dry leaf per 8 ounces of water, and use an infuser basket. For a stronger infusion, add another teaspoonful or two of dry tea leaf.

TIME

As soon as the water reaches the correct temperature for the type of tea, pour it over the leaves or tea bag in the teapot, and cover the pot with a lid. Set a timer—usually 1 to 2 minutes for whites and oolongs; 2 to 3 minutes for greens; and 3 to 5 minutes for blacks, puerhs, and herbals. (Steeping tea longer than recommended can yield a bitter infusion.) When the timer goes off, remove the infuser basket or the tea bags from the teapot.

ENJOYMENT

For best flavor, serve the tea as soon as possible. Keep the beverage warm atop a lighted warmer or under your favorite tea cozy if necessary.

Tea-Pairing Guide

CHOOSING A TEA that perfectly complements the menu for afternoon tea is a critical part of hosting a successful event. When selecting infusions, especially to pair with sweets, bear in mind that the flavor of the tea should enhance—rather than compete with or overpower—the flavors of the food, and vice versa. For that reason, we recommend reserving delicate teas, such as the whites, for drinking on their own, unless they are flavored with fruit or flowers. Green teas, in general, are best enjoyed with savory dishes, though there are a few exceptions to that rule. Because desserts are typically sweet and buttery, black teas and oolong teas are excellent choices. The following guide offers recommendations of teas to pair with the various flavor profiles of sweets in this book, but it should by no means be considered definitive:

BERRIES Madame Butterfly Jasmine Green Tea, Darjeeling 1st Flush Black Tea, China Milk Oolong Tea

CHOCOLATE Golden Monkey Black Tea, Keemun Spring Mao Feng Black Tea, Duke Cardiff Blend Black Tea

CITRUS Fujian Ti Kuan Yin Oolong Tea, Phoenix Mountain Oolong Tea, Darjeeling Ambootia Black Tea

MINT Keemun Hao Ya A Black Tea, Darjeeling 2nd Flush Black Tea

NUTS Nepal Mist Valley Black Tea, Da Hong Pao Oolong Tea, Vietnam Imperial Oolong Tea

SPICES Nepal Ilam Black Tea, Assam Belseri Black Tea, Nilgiri Frost Black Tea

OTHER FRUITS Golden Monkey Black Tea, Fancy Formosa Oolong Tea, Yunnan Golden Tips Black Tea

TROPICAL FRUITS Oriental Beauty Oolong Tea, Luan Guapian Green Tea, Jade Oolong Tea

VANILLA Cream Earl Grey Black Tea, Ceylon Blackwood Estate Black Tea, Taiwanese Gui Fei Oolong Tea

A prudent host will prepare the chosen tea in advance of the event to verify that the pairing is pleasing and to determine the most beneficial water temperature and steep time. This will ensure good tea and a delightful teatime.

Cakes & Cupcakes

INDIVIDUAL CHOCOLATE-
BANANA BUNDT CAKES
(recipe on page 22)

Coconut-Lime Cakes

Yield: 15 servings | Preparation: 25 minutes
Bake: 15 to 16 minutes | Cool: 1 hour | Freeze: 1 hour

2½ cups plus 5 tablespoons sifted cake flour,
   such as Swans Down
1 tablespoon fresh lime zest
2 teaspoons baking powder
½ teaspoon baking soda
½ teaspoon salt
1 cup salted butter, softened
1¾ cups sugar
4 large eggs
1½ teaspoons coconut extract
½ teaspoon vanilla extract
1 cup whole buttermilk
1 recipe Lime Buttercream (recipe follows)
Garnish: chopped roasted, salted macadamias
   and toasted, shredded sweetened coconut

• Preheat oven to 350°.
• Spray a 18-x-13-inch rimmed baking sheet with
nonstick cooking spray. Line with parchment paper,
and spray again. Set aside.
• In a medium bowl, combine flour, lime zest, baking
powder, baking soda, and salt, whisking well. Set aside.
• In a large mixing bowl, beat butter at medium speed
with an electric mixer until creamy. Gradually add
sugar, beating until light and fluffy, approximately 3
minutes. Add eggs, one at a time, beating well after
each addition. Add coconut extract and vanilla extract.
• Add flour mixture to butter mixture in thirds, alternately with buttermilk, beginning and ending with flour.
Pour batter into prepared pan, and spread evenly. Tap
pan sharply on countertop to reduce air bubbles.
• Bake until a wooden pick inserted in the center comes
out clean, 15 to 16 minutes. Let cool in pan on a wire rack.
• When completely cool, remove from pan, and cut
into 2 (13-x-9-inch) portions. Spread Lime Buttercream
evenly over each portion. Stack 1 portion on top of
the other. Freeze until firm, approximately 1 hour.
• Trim crusts from edges. Cut into 2½-inch squares.
• Garnish with chopped macadamias and toasted
coconut.
• Let come to room temperature before serving, if
desired.

*Make-Ahead Tip: Cake can be baked in advance,
frosted and assembled, wrapped securely in plastic wrap,
and frozen for up to a week. Cut while frozen. Let thaw
before garnishing and serving.*

*Kitchen Tip: To create clean cuts, use a long, sharp
knife, and press downward.*

Lime Buttercream

Yield: 2½ cups | Preparation: 10 minutes

1 cup butter, softened
4 cups confectioners' sugar
1 teaspoon fresh lime zest
2 tablespoons fresh lime juice

• In a large mixing bowl, combine butter, confectioners' sugar, lime zest, and lime juice. Beat at medium
speed with an electric mixer, gradually increasing to
high speed, until smooth and creamy.
• Use immediately.

*Make-Ahead Tip: Lime Buttercream can be made a
day in advance, covered, and refrigerated until needed.
Let come to room temperature before spreading.*

Almond-Apple Tea Bread *(photo on page 17)*

Yield: 3 mini loaves | Preparation: 30 minutes
Bake: 40 to 43 minutes | Cool: 1 hour

½ cup superfine or castor sugar
½ cup all-purpose flour
½ cup ground slivered almonds
¼ teaspoon salt
4 large egg whites
½ cup salted butter, melted
½ cup diced peeled apple
¼ teaspoon apple pie spice
Garnish: confectioners' sugar

• Preheat oven to 350°.
• Spray 3 (6-x-3¼-inch) mini loaf pans with nonstick
baking spray with flour. Set aside.
• In a large bowl, combine sugar, flour, almonds,
and salt, whisking well. Add egg whites, stirring until
incorporated. Add melted butter, stirring well. Divide
mixture evenly among prepared loaf pans. Sprinkle
apples evenly over batter. Sprinkle apple pie spice
evenly over apples.
• Bake loaves until tops are golden and a wooden
pick inserted in the centers comes out clean, 40 to 43
minutes. Let cool in pans for 5 minutes. Remove from
pans, and transfer to a wire rack. Let cool completely.
• Garnish with confectioners' sugar, if desired.

*Make-Ahead Tip: These breads are best on the day
they are made, but they will keep for a few days wrapped
securely in plastic wrap.*

*Editor's Note: There is no leavening in this recipe.
The loaves are dense yet moist and have a fine crumb.*

ALMOND-APPLE TEA BREAD
(recipe on page 16)

Kitchen Tip:
To serve, cut thin slices, using a sharp, serrated bread knife.

Spice Cakes with Lemon Cream

Yield: 12 servings | *Preparation: 20 minutes*
Bake: 18 minutes | *Cool: 1 hour*

2 cups all-purpose flour
1 teaspoon baking powder
½ teaspoon ground cinnamon
½ teaspoon ground ginger
¼ teaspoon ground mace
¼ teaspoon salt
⅛ teaspoon ground cloves
⅛ teaspoon ground black pepper
⅛ teaspoon ground nutmeg
4 large eggs
⅓ cup sour cream
⅓ cup unsulfured molasses, such as Grandma's
1½ teaspoons vanilla extract
1 cup salted butter, softened
1¼ cups firmly packed light brown sugar
2 teaspoons fresh lemon zest
1 recipe Lemon Cream (recipe follows)
Garnish: sugared thyme and red grapes

- Preheat oven to 350°.
- Spray a 13-x-9-inch baking pan with nonstick cooking spray with flour. Set aside.
- In a medium bowl, combine flour, baking powder, cinnamon, ginger, mace, salt, cloves, pepper, and nutmeg, whisking well. Set aside.
- In a small bowl, combine eggs, sour cream, molasses, and vanilla extract, whisking to incorporate. Set aside.
- In a large mixing bowl, combine butter, brown sugar, and lemon zest. Beat at high speed with an electric mixer until light and fluffy, approximately 3 minutes. Add egg mixture, beating at low speed until combined. Add flour mixture, beating at low speed until combined. Beat at medium speed for 2 minutes.
- Spread batter into prepared pan, creating a smooth and level surface. Tap pan forcefully on counter 2 to 3 times to remove air bubbles.
- Bake until a wooden pick inserted in the center comes out clean, 18 to 20 minutes. Let cool completely in pan on a wire rack.
- Using a 2½-inch round cutter, cut 12 circles from cake. Spread Lemon Cream on tops of cakes.
- Garnish with sugared thyme and grapes, if desired.
- Serve immediately.

Make-Ahead Tip: Cake circles can be frozen in an airtight container for up to a week in advance. Thaw before topping with Lemon Cream.

Kitchen Tip: To make sugared thyme, spray thyme sprigs with nonstick cooking spray, and dust with superfine sugar.

Lemon Cream

Yield: 1½ cups | *Preparation: 5 minutes*

1 cup cold heavy whipping cream
2 tablespoons confectioners' sugar
3 tablespoons prepared lemon curd

- In a medium mixing bowl, combine cream and confectioners' sugar. Beat at high speed with an electric mixer until thickened and creamy. Set aside.
- In a small bowl, stir lemon curd vigorously with a spoon. Add curd to whipped cream, beating at high speed just until incorporated.
- Refrigerate in an airtight container for up to a day.

Let cool in pans for 5 minutes. Transfer to a wire rack, and let cool completely.
• Place Buttercream Frosting in a piping bag fitted with a medium open-star tip (Wilton #21). Pipe frosting onto cooled cupcakes.
• Refrigerate cupcakes, covered, until ready to serve.
• Garnish with lavender petals just before serving, if desired.

Make-Ahead Tip: Cupcakes can be made in advance and frozen (unfrosted) in an airtight container for up to a week. Let thaw before frosting.

Buttercream Frosting

Yield: 1½ cups | Preparation: 15 minutes

¾ cup salted butter, softened
2½ cups confectioners' sugar
2 tablespoons plus 2 teaspoons whole milk

• In a large mixing bowl, beat butter at high speed with an electric mixer until creamy. Add confectioners' sugar and milk, starting at low speed and gradually increasing to high speed. Beat until light and creamy.
• Use immediately.

Peanut Butter Pound Cake

Yield: 12 to 16 servings | Preparation: 40 minutes
Bake: 53 to 55 minutes | Cool: 1 hour

½ cup salted butter, softened
½ cup creamy peanut butter
1½ cups sugar
1¼ teaspoons vanilla extract
3 large eggs, at room temperature
1½ cups sifted cake flour, such as Swans Down
¼ teaspoon baking powder
¼ teaspoon salt
½ cup whole milk
1 recipe Peanut Butter Frosting (recipe follows)
Garnish: chopped peanuts

• Preheat oven to 350°.
• Spray a 6-cup Bundt pan* with nonstick baking spray with flour. Set aside.
• In a large mixing bowl, beat butter at medium-high speed with an electric mixer until creamy. Add peanut butter, sugar, and vanilla extract, beating until light and fluffy, approximately 3 minutes. Add eggs, one at a time, beating well after each addition. Set aside.
• In a medium bowl, combine flour, baking powder, and salt, whisking well. Add flour mixture to peanut-butter

Orange-Lavender Mini Cupcakes

Yield: 40 mini cupcakes | Preparation: 35 minutes
Bake: 12 to 14 minutes | Cool: 30 minutes

½ cup salted butter, softened
1 cup sugar
2 large eggs
¼ teaspoon orange extract
1½ cups all-purpose flour
1 tablespoon fresh orange zest
1½ teaspoons dried culinary lavender,
   such as McCormick's
½ teaspoon baking powder
¼ teaspoon salt
⅔ cup whole milk
1 recipe Buttercream Frosting (recipe follows)
Garnish: lavender petals

• Preheat oven to 350°.
• Line 40 wells of 2 (24-well) mini muffin pans with paper liners. Set aside.
• In a large mixing bowl, beat butter at high speed with an electric mixer until creamy. Gradually add sugar, beating until light and fluffy, approximately 5 minutes. Add eggs, one at a time, beating well after each addition. Add orange extract, beating to combine. Set aside.
• In a medium bowl, combine flour, orange zest, lavender, baking powder, and salt, whisking well. Add half of flour mixture to butter mixture, beating at low speed. Add milk and remaining flour mixture, beating to incorporate.
• Using a levered 1-tablespoon scoop, drop batter into baking cups.
• Bake until a wooden pick inserted in the centers of cupcakes comes out clean, approximately 12 minutes.

*We used NordicWare's 6-cup Anniversary Cast Bundt Pan, which is available at nordicware.com.

mixture in thirds, alternately with milk, beginning and ending with flour. Place batter in prepared pan, filling no more than three-quarters, and smooth evenly. Rap pan on the countertop several times to settle batter and reduce air bubbles.

• Bake until a wooden pick inserted near the center comes out clean, 53 to 55 minutes. (Cake will have a high dome but will not spill out of pan). Let cake cool in pan for 10 minutes. Using a long, serrated knife, trim dome off of cake so cake will sit level when inverted. Invert cake onto a wire rack, and let cool completely.

• Place Peanut Butter Frosting in a resealable plastic bag with a corner snipped off to make a small opening. Pipe frosting onto cooled cake in a decorative fashion.

• Garnish with chopped peanuts, if desired.

Peanut Butter Frosting
Yield: 1 cup | Preparation: 10 minutes

¼ cup creamy peanut butter
¼ cup light corn syrup
1 cup confectioners' sugar
2 teaspoons whole milk
½ teaspoon vanilla extract

• In a small saucepan, combine peanut butter and corn syrup. Cook over low heat, stirring until smooth and creamy. Remove from heat, and add confectioners' sugar, milk, and vanilla extract, stirring until incorporated.

• Use immediately.

Blueberry Buckle

Yield: 16 servings | Preparation: 15 minutes
Bake: 40 minutes

1¾ cups all-purpose flour
2 teaspoons baking powder
½ teaspoon salt
¼ teaspoon ground cinnamon
¼ teaspoon ground nutmeg
½ cup salted butter, softened
¾ cup sugar
1 large egg
½ cup whole milk
1 teaspoon vanilla extract
2 cups fresh blueberries
1 recipe Streusel (recipe follows)
Garnish: confectioners' sugar and fresh blueberries

• Preheat oven to 375°.
• Line the bottom and sides of an 8-inch square baking pan with aluminum foil, letting foil hang over sides at least 1 inch. Coat with nonstick cooking spray. Set aside.
• In a medium bowl, combine flour, baking powder, salt, cinnamon, and nutmeg, whisking well. Set aside.
• In a large bowl, combine butter and sugar, stirring vigorously with a wooden spoon until creamy. Add egg, stirring well until incorporated. Set aside.
• In a small bowl, combine milk and vanilla extract. Add flour mixture and milk mixture to butter mixture, stirring until well combined. Add blueberries, gently folding in.
• Spread batter into prepared pan, and sprinkle Streusel over top.
• Bake until a wooden pick inserted in the center comes out clean, approximately 40 minutes. Let cool in pan on a wire rack until slightly warm.
• Lift buckle from pan, using foil overhang as handles. Place on a cutting board, and cut into 16 squares. Remove any aluminum foil that may have stuck to buckle squares.
• Serve warm or at room temperature.
• Garnish with confectioners' sugar and fresh blueberries, if desired.

Make-Ahead Tip: *Blueberry Buckle can be made in advance and frozen for up to 1 week. Or it can be made a day ahead, covered, and stored at room temperature.*

Streusel

Yield: approximately ¾ cup | Preparation: 5 minutes

½ cup firmly packed light brown sugar
¼ cup quick-cooking oats
2 tablespoons all-purpose flour
½ teaspoon ground cinnamon
½ teaspoon ground nutmeg
⅛ teaspoon salt
3 tablespoons cold salted butter, cut into ½-inch pieces

• In a bowl, combine brown sugar, oats, flour, cinnamon, nutmeg, and salt. Using a pastry blender, cut butter into oat mixture until mixture resembles coarse crumbs.

Individual Chocolate-Banana Bundt Cakes *(photo on page 23)*

Yield: 10 individual cakes | Preparation: 25 minutes
Bake: 17 to 19 minutes | Cool: 30 minutes

2 ounces unsweetened baking chocolate
1 cups all-purpose flour
¼ teaspoon baking soda
⅛ teaspoon salt
½ cup salted butter, softened
¾ cup sugar
1 large egg
½ teaspoon vanilla extract
¼ cup whole buttermilk
⅓ cup mashed ripe banana
Garnish: confectioners' sugar

• Preheat oven to 325°.
• Spray 10 wells of 2 (6-well) swirled Bundt pans* with nonstick baking spray with flour. Set aside.
• Melt chocolate according to package instructions. Set aside.
• In a medium bowl, combine flour, baking soda, and salt, whisking well. Set aside.
• In a large mixing bowl, combine butter and sugar. Beat at medium speed with an electric mixer until creamy, approximately 3 minutes. Add egg, beating well. Add vanilla extract, beating until bended. Add flour mixture to butter mixture in thirds, alternately with buttermilk, beginning and ending with flour mixture. Add banana and melted chocolate, beating just until incorporated.
• Using a levered ¼-cup scoop, divide batter evenly among prepared wells of pans. Tap pan forcefully on counter several times to settle batter and to remove air bubbles.
• Bake until a wooden pick inserted in the centers comes out clean, approximately 17 to 19 minutes. Let cool in pans for 10 minutes. Transfer to a wire rack, and let cool completely.
• Garnish with a dusting of confectioners' sugar before serving, if desired.

We used a Nordicware Anniversary Bundtlette Pan, which is available at nordicware.com.

INDIVIDUAL CHOCOLATE-
BANANA BUNDT CAKES
(recipe on page 22)

Make-Ahead Tip: *Cakes can be baked a week in advance and frozen in an airtight container. Let thaw completely before dusting with confectioners' sugar.*

Red Velvet Mini Cupcakes

Yield: 48 mini cupcakes | Preparation: 30 minutes
Bake: 13 to 14 minutes | Cool: 30 minutes

1¼ cups sifted cake flour, such as Swans Down
1 tablespoon plus 2 teaspoons natural unsweetened
　 cocoa powder
¼ teaspoon baking powder
¼ teaspoon salt
¼ cup salted butter, softened
¾ cup sugar
1 large egg
1 teaspoon vanilla extract
½ cup whole buttermilk
1 tablespoon liquid red food coloring
½ teaspoon white vinegar
½ teaspoon baking soda
1 recipe Vanilla Buttercream (recipe follows)
Garnish: White Chocolate Hearts and red sprinkles
　 (nonpareils), such as Wilton

- Preheat oven to 350°.
- Line 2 (24-well) mini muffin pans with cupcake liners.
Set aside.
- In a medium bowl, combine flour, cocoa powder,
baking powder, and salt, whisking well. Set aside.
- In a large mixing bowl, beat butter at medium speed
with an electric mixer until soft and creamy, approximately 1 minute. Gradually add sugar, beating at high
speed until light and fluffy, approximately 3 minutes.
Add egg, beating until incorporated. Add vanilla
extract, beating until incorporated. Set aside.
- In a liquid measuring cup, combine buttermilk and
red food coloring, whisking to blend. Add flour mixture
to butter mixture in thirds, alternately with buttermilk
mixture, beginning and ending with flour mixture.
Beat until incorporated.
- In a small bowl, combine vinegar and baking soda,
stirring until mixture fizzes. Quickly add mixture to
cake batter, beating at low speed just until incorporated. Working quickly and using a levered 2-teaspoon
scoop, divide batter evenly among wells of prepared
muffin pans.
- Bake until a wooden pick inserted in the centers
comes out clean, 13 to 14 minutes. Let cupcakes cool
in pans for 5 minutes. Transfer to a wire rack, and let
cool completely.
- Place Vanilla Buttercream in a piping bag fitted with
a large open-star tip (Wilton #1). Pipe a decorative swirl
on tops of cupcakes.
- Store, covered, in the refrigerator until serving time.
- Just before serving, garnish each cupcake with a
White Chocolate Heart and red sprinkles, if desired.

Vanilla Buttercream

Yield: 2½ cups | Preparation: 10 minutes

1 cup salted butter, softened
4 cups confectioners' sugar
3 tablespoons whole milk
½ teaspoon vanilla extract

- In a large mixing bowl, combine butter, confectioners'
sugar, milk, and vanilla extract. Beat with an electric
mixer, starting at low speed and gradually increasing
to high speed, until smooth and creamy.
- Use immediately.

White Chocolate Hearts

Yield: 48 hearts | Preparation: 20 minutes

1½ (4-ounce) bars white chocolate, such as Ghirardelli
Red sprinkles (nonpareils), such as Wilton

- Line a rimmed baking sheet with waxed paper. Set aside.
- Melt white chocolate according to package directions.
Working quickly and using an offset spatula, spread
melted chocolate onto prepared baking sheet in an
even layer approximately ¼ inch thick. Evenly distribute sprinkles over melted chocolate. Refrigerate until
chocolate is firm, approximately 1 hour.
- Using a 1-inch heart-shaped cutter*, cut shapes from
chilled chocolate. Refrigerate until needed.

We used a heart-shaped linzer cutter.

Cream Cheese Frosting

Yield: 2½ cups | Preparation: 5 minutes

½ cup salted butter, softened
1 (8-ounce) package cream cheese, softened
1 (1-pound) box confectioners' sugar
1 teaspoon vanilla extract

• In a large mixing bowl, combine butter, cream cheese, confectioners' sugar, and vanilla extract. Beat at medium speed with an electric mixer until smooth.
• Use immediately.

Sweet Remembrances
continuing a legacy

Nancy Reppert's mother, Bertha, was ahead of her time. She opened an herb shop called the Rosemary House in Mechanicsburg, Pennsylvania, in 1968, long before the mainstream public realized the culinary and medicinal values of fresh herbs. "My mother was renowned throughout the world of herbs," recalls Nancy, who worked in her mother's shop throughout her teenage years.

In 1990, when the red brick row house next door to the Rosemary House became available, Nancy opened Sweet Remembrances, a tearoom extension of her mother's business. (Nancy's sister, Susanna, now runs the Rosemary House.) Sweet Remembrances is open every Wednesday for afternoon tea, as well as the first Saturday of each month. Nancy does all the cooking herself, and she always serves everything piping hot—never reheated. She honors her mother's legacy by incorporating fresh herbs and edible flowers from the garden that grows just outside her kitchen door. Cooking is Nancy's favorite part of her job, as well as coming up with the delicious menus that feature many locally sourced organic foods. Regardless of the menu, patrons can be assured of enjoying "a bottomless pot of properly brewed loose-leaf tea," selected from among the 40 varieties of teas Sweet Remembrances offers.

"Sweet Remembrances and the Rosemary House are really a family affair," Nancy points out. "My sister and I work very closely together, and my sister's daughter, my niece, now works as a waitress at Sweet Remembrances." The customers who patronize both businesses see the family relationship. "That's one of the things they appreciate about us," Nancy says.

Carrot Cake Mini Cupcakes
Yield: approximately 72 mini cupcakes
Preparation: 40 minutes | Bake: 15 minutes
Cool: 30 minutes

1½ cups vegetable oil
1½ cups sugar
4 large eggs, well beaten
1 pound carrots, peeled and finely grated
2 cups unbleached all-purpose flour
2 teaspoons baking soda
2 teaspoons ground cinnamon
½ teaspoon salt
½ teaspoon ground nutmeg
¼ teaspoon ground cloves
¼ teaspoon ground mace
1 cup finely chopped walnuts
1 cup golden raisins
1 teaspoon vanilla extract
1 recipe Cream Cheese Frosting (recipe opposite)
Garnish: edible flowers*

• Preheat oven to 325°.
• Line 3 (24-well) mini muffin pans with paper liners. Set aside.
• In a large mixing bowl, combine oil and sugar. Add eggs and carrots, stirring to combine. Set aside.
• In another bowl, combine flour, baking soda, cinnamon, salt, nutmeg, cloves, and mace, whisking well. Add flour mixture to carrot mixture, stirring to combine. Add walnuts, raisins, and vanilla extract, stirring gently to blend. Divide batter evenly among wells of prepared muffin pans.
• Bake until a wooden pick inserted in the centers comes out clean, approximately 15 minutes. Remove cupcakes from pans, and let cool completely on wire racks.
• Place Cream Cheese Frosting in a piping bag fitted with a large open-star tip (Ateco #848). Pipe frosting onto cooled cupcakes. Refrigerate until serving time.
• Garnish with edible flowers, if desired.

We used edible flowers from Gourmet Sweet Botanicals, 800-931-7530, gourmetsweetbotanicals.com.

White Chocolate–Lemon Cake

Yield: 24 servings | Preparation: 30 minutes
Bake: 11 to 13 minutes | Cool: 1 hour

1 (15.25-ounce) white cake mix
3 large eggs
1 cup water
¼ cup vegetable oil
⅓ cup sour cream
1 tablespoon fresh lemon zest
1 recipe Lemon-Mascarpone Filling (recipe follows)
1 recipe Lemon–White Chocolate Buttercream
  (recipe follows)
Garnish: lemon curls and fresh mint

• Preheat oven to 350°.
• Spray an 18-x-13-inch rimmed baking sheet with
nonstick cooking spray. Line with parchment paper,
and spray again. Set aside.
• In a large mixing bowl, combine cake mix, eggs, water,
oil, sour cream, and lemon zest. Beat at low speed with
an electric mixer for 30 seconds, scraping down sides of
bowl as necessary. Increase speed to medium, and beat
for 2 minutes. Spread batter into prepared pan.
• Bake until light golden brown and a wooden pick
inserted in the center comes out clean, 11 to 13 minutes. Let cake cool completely in pan on a wire rack.
• Remove cake from pan, and place on a cutting
surface. Cut cake into 2 (13-x-9-inch) portions. Spread
Lemon-Mascarpone Filling on one portion. Top with
remaining cake portion. Spread top with Lemon–White
Chocolate Buttercream. Using a sharp serrated knife,
trim sides of cake, discarding crusts. Cut into 2½-x-1-
inch pieces.
• Store cakes in a covered container in the refrigerator.
• Garnish with lemon curls and fresh mint just before
serving, if desired.

Kitchen Tip: *To make cake easier to cut, place in freezer
for approximately 30 minutes.*

Lemon-Mascarpone Filling

Yield: 2 cups | Preparation: 5 minutes

1 (10-ounce) jar lemon curd, such as Dickinson's
1 (8-ounce) carton mascarpone cheese

• In a small bowl, stir lemon curd vigorously to loosen.
Add mascarpone cheese, stirring until combined. Use
immediately, or refrigerate in a covered container until
needed.

Lemon–White Chocolate Buttercream

Yield: 3 cups | Preparation: 20 minutes

1 cup salted butter, softened
3½ cups confectioners' sugar
1 teaspoon lemon zest
2 tablespoons fresh lemon juice
½ teaspoon lemon extract
½ teaspoon salt
1 (4-ounce) bar white chocolate, melted and cooled,
  such as Ghirardelli

• In a large mixing bowl, combine butter, confectioners'
sugar, lemon zest, lemon juice, lemon extract, and salt.
Beat with an electric mixer, starting at low speed and
gradually increasing to high speed. Add white chocolate, beating until incorporated.
• Use immediately, or refrigerate in a covered container
until needed. Let come to room temperature to soften,
and beat with an electric mixer for 1 minute before using.

Vanilla–Sour Cream Tea Bread *(photo on page 29)*

Yield: 2 mini loaves | Preparation: 20 minutes
Bake: 30 to 33 minutes | Cool: 30 minutes

1½ cups all-purpose flour
¾ cup sugar
2 teaspoons baking powder
½ teaspoon baking soda
¼ teaspoon salt
½ cup sour cream
¼ cup salted butter, melted
2 large eggs
2 teaspoons vanilla, butter, and nut flavoring,
  such as McCormick's

• Preheat oven to 350°.
• Spray 2 (6-x-3¼-inch) mini loaf pans with nonstick
baking spray with flour. Set aside.
• In a medium bowl, combine flour, sugar, baking
powder, baking soda, and salt, whisking well. Set aside.
• In a small bowl, combine sour cream; melted butter;
eggs; and vanilla, butter, and nut flavoring, stirring
well. Add to flour mixture, stirring just until wet
ingredients are incorporated. (Batter will be stiff.)
• Divide batter evenly among prepared pans,
smoothing with an offset spatula.
• Bake until loaves are light golden brown and a
wooden pick inserted in the centers comes out clean,
30 to 33 minutes. Remove from pans, and let cool
completely on wire racks.
• Wrap tightly in plastic wrap, or store in an airtight
container for up to 2 days.

VANILLA-SOUR CREAM TEA BREAD (recipe on page 27)

- Preheat oven to 350°.
- Line an 18-x-13-inch rimmed baking sheet with parchment paper, and spray with nonstick cooking spray. Set aside.
- In a medium bowl, combine flour, baking powder, salt, and baking soda, whisking well. Set aside.
- In a large mixing bowl, beat butter at high speed with an electric mixer until creamy. Add sugar, and beat until light and fluffy, approximately 4 minutes. Add jam. Add eggs, one at a time, beating well after each addition. Add vanilla extract and food coloring (to achieve desired color), beating to combine.
- With mixer on low speed, add flour mixture to butter mixture in thirds, alternately with buttermilk, beginning and ending with flour mixture. Beat until combined.
- Pour batter into prepared pan, and spread evenly. Tap pan several times on countertop to reduce air bubbles in batter.
- Bake on middle rack of oven until a wooden pick inserted in the center comes out clean, approximately 15 minutes.
- Let cake cool completely in pan on a wire rack. Freeze for 1 hour.
- Using a 2-inch round cutter, cut 34 circles from cake.
- Place Strawberry–Cream Cheese Frosting in a pastry bag fitted with a large open-star tip (Wilton #1M). Pipe frosting onto 17 cake circles. Refrigerate for 15 minutes.
- Top each cake circle with another cake circle, and pipe frosting onto top. Refrigerate for at least 15 minutes or until needed.
- Garnish each with a strawberry rosette just before serving, if desired.

Strawberry Jam Cakes

Yield: 17 servings | Preparation: 45 minutes
Bake: 15 minutes | Cool: 1 hour
Freeze: 1 hour | Refrigerate: 30 minutes

2 cups sifted cake flour, such as Swans Down
1 teaspoon baking powder
½ teaspoon salt
¼ teaspoon baking soda
½ cup salted butter, softened
1¼ cups sugar
½ cup seedless strawberry jam
3 large eggs
½ teaspoon vanilla extract
Red food coloring paste
⅓ cup whole buttermilk
1 recipe Strawberry–Cream Cheese Frosting
 (recipe follows)
Garnish: fresh strawberry rosettes*

Strawberry–Cream Cheese Frosting

Yield: 2½ cups | Preparation: 10 minutes
Refrigerate: 30 minutes

4 ounces cream cheese, softened
½ cup salted butter, softened
2 tablespoons seedless strawberry jam
½ teaspoon vanilla extract
3½ cups confectioners' sugar
Red food coloring paste (optional)

- In a large mixing bowl, combine cream cheese, butter, jam, vanilla extract, and confectioners' sugar. Beat at low speed with an electric mixer until incorporated. Increase speed to high, and beat until frosting is light and fluffy, 2 to 3 minutes.
- If desired, tint frosting with food coloring, beating until uniform.
- Refrigerate for 30 minutes before using.

*HOW-TO
on page 128

Make-Ahead Tip: Cake layers can be made a week in advance, wrapped securely in plastic wrap, and frozen until needed. Let layers thaw completely before frosting.

Fresh Raspberry Cake

Yield: 16 servings | Preparation: 45 minutes
Bake: 15 minutes | Cool: 1 hour

1¾ cups sifted cake flour, such as Swans Down
1¾ teaspoons baking powder
¼ teaspoon salt
½ cup salted butter, softened
1 cup sugar
½ cup whole milk
¾ teaspoon vanilla extract
4 large egg whites
1 recipe Fresh Raspberry–Cream Cheese Frosting
   (recipe follows)
Garnish: fresh raspberries and fresh mint

• Preheat oven to 350°.
• Spray 2 (9-inch) round cake pans with nonstick baking spray with flour. Set aside.
• In a medium bowl, combine flour, baking powder, and salt, whisking well. Set aside.
• In a large mixing bowl, beat butter at high speed with an electric mixer until creamy. Gradually add sugar, beating until light and fluffy, 3 to 5 minutes. Set aside.
• In a liquid measuring cup, combine milk and vanilla extract, stirring to blend. Add flour mixture to butter mixture in thirds, alternately with milk mixture, beginning and ending with flour mixture. Set aside.
• In a medium mixing bowl, beat egg whites at high speed until stiff peaks form. Gently fold into cake batter in thirds. Divide cake batter evenly between prepared pans. Tap cake pans gently on countertop to level and reduce air bubbles.
• Bake until edges of layers are golden brown and a wooden pick inserted in the centers comes out clean, 13 to15 minutes. Let cool in pans for 10 minutes. Invert layers onto wire racks, and let cool completely.
• Place 1 cake layer on a cake plate. Spread Fresh Raspberry–Cream Cheese Frosting on top. Top with another cake layer (either bottom sides together or top sides together). Spread frosting over top and sides of cake, swirling with an offset spatula to create a decorative pattern.
• Store cake, covered, in the refrigerator for up to 3 days.
• Garnish with raspberries and mint just before serving, if desired.

Fresh Raspberry–Cream Cheese Frosting

Yield: 2¼ cups | Preparation: 15 minutes
Refrigerate: 8 hours or overnight

¼ cup salted butter, softened
4 ounces cream cheese, softened
4 cups confectioners' sugar
⅛ teaspoon salt
½ teaspoon vanilla extract
½ cup fresh raspberries

• In a large mixing bowl, combine butter and cream cheese. Beat at high speed with an electric mixer until blended and smooth. Add confectioners' sugar, salt, and vanilla extract, beating until smooth and creamy, Add raspberries, beating at low speed until well blended. Refrigerate in an airtight container until needed.

" Whence could it have come to me, this all-powerful joy? I was conscious that it was connected with the taste of the tea and the cake…"

Marcel Proust,
Remembrance of Things Past

GLUTEN FREE

Flourless Hazelnut Torte with Apricot Preserves

Yield: 12 to 14 servings | *Preparation: 30 minutes*
Bake: 27 to 29 minutes | *Cool: 1 hour*

1¼ cups whole raw hazelnuts with skins
4 large eggs, separated
¾ cup superfine or castor sugar
¼ teaspoon vanilla extract
¼ teaspoon salt
1 (10-ounce) jar apricot preserves, such as Dickinson's

• Preheat oven to 350°.
• Spray a 9-inch round springform pan with nonstick cooking spray. Set aside.
• In the work bowl of a food processor, pulse hazelnuts until finely ground, being careful not to overprocess into a nut butter. Set aside.
• In a large mixing bowl, combine egg yolks and sugar. Beat at high speed with an electric mixer until light and creamy, approximately 2 minutes. Add vanilla extract, stirring to combine. Set aside.
• Add salt to hazelnuts, whisking well. Add hazelnut mixture to egg yolk mixture, beating at medium speed until incorporated. (Batter will be very stiff.) Set aside.
• In another mixing bowl, beat egg whites at high speed with an electric mixer until stiff peaks form. Spoon one-third of beaten egg whites into hazelnut batter, stirring vigorously to loosen mixture. Add remaining egg whites, folding to incorporate. Spread mixture into prepared pan, smoothing with an offset spatula.
• Bake until torte is golden brown and a wooden pick inserted in the center comes out clean, 27 to 29 minutes. (Top of torte should feel somewhat firm to the touch, and edges should be golden brown.) Let torte cool completely in pan, approximately 1 hour.
• Using a sharp knife or a thin offset spatula, loosen sides of torte from pan before removing sides of pan. In the same manner, loosen torte from bottom of pan. Place torte on a cake plate.
• In a small saucepan, melt apricot preserves over low heat, stirring to loosen. Spoon preserves over surface of torte, spreading evenly.

Make-Ahead Tip: *Flourless Hazelnut Torte can be made in advance, wrapped tightly in plastic wrap, and frozen for up to 1 week. Let thaw before spreading apricot preserves over torte.*

Spiced Plum Bundt Cake *(photo on page 35)*

Yield: 12 to 16 servings | *Preparation: 30 minutes*
Bake: 50 to 52 minutes | *Cool: 1 hour*

½ cup chopped dried plums
1 cup salted butter, softened
1 cup sugar
3 large eggs, at room temperature
½ teaspoon vanilla extract
2 cups sifted cake flour, such as Swans Down
1 teaspoon ground cinnamon
¼ teaspoon baking soda
¼ teaspoon salt
½ cup sour cream
⅓ cup chopped toasted walnuts
Garnish: confectioners' sugar

• Preheat oven to 325°.
• Spray a 6-cup Bundt pan* with nonstick baking spray with flour. Set aside.
• Place dried plums in a small bowl, and cover with very hot water. Let stand for 5 minutes to rehydrate. Drain well. Set plums aside.
• In a large mixing bowl, beat butter at high speed with an electric mixer until creamy. Add sugar, beating until light and fluffy, approximately 5 minutes. Add eggs, one at a time, beating well after each addition. Add vanilla extract, beating until incorporated. Set aside.
• In a medium bowl, combine cake flour, cinnamon, baking soda, and salt, whisking well. With mixer at low speed, add flour mixture to butter mixture in thirds, alternately with sour cream, beginning and ending with flour mixture. Add rehydrated plums and walnuts, stirring to combine. (Batter will be thick.) Place batter in prepared pan, filling no more than three-quarters, and spread evenly. Smooth top with a spatula, and tap cake pan firmly on countertop several times to settle batter and reduce air bubbles.
• Bake until a wooden pick inserted in the center comes out clean, 50 to 52 minutes. Let cake cool in pan for 10 minutes. Using a long, serrated knife, trim dome off of cake so cake will sit level when inverted. Invert cake onto a wire rack, and let cool completely.
• Garnish with a dusting of confectioners' sugar, if desired.

*We used Nordicware's 6-cup Anniversary Cast Bundt Pan, which is available at nordicware.com.

Make-Ahead Tip: *Cake can be baked in advance, wrapped securely in plastic wrap, and frozen (ungarnished) for up to a week. Let cake thaw completely before garnishing with confectioners' sugar.*

SPICED PLUM BUNDT CAKE
(recipe on page 34)

Italian Cream Cupcakes

Yield: 17 cupcakes | Preparation: 45 minutes
Bake: 16 to 18 minutes | Cool: 30 minutes

½ cup salted butter, softened
1 cup sugar
2 large eggs
¼ cup sour cream
¼ cup whole milk
1 teaspoon vanilla extract
1½ cups sifted cake flour, such as Swans Down
1½ teaspoons baking powder
⅛ teaspoon salt
½ cup finely chopped sweetened, flaked coconut*
¼ cup finely chopped toasted pecans
1 recipe Italian Cream Cheese Frosting (recipe follows)
Garnish: chopped, toasted pecans

• Preheat oven to 350°.
• Line 17 wells of 2 (12-well) muffin pans with paper liners. Set aside.
• In a large mixing bowl, beat butter at medium speed with an electric mixer until creamy. Gradually add sugar, beating until light and fluffy, approximately 3 minutes. Add eggs, one at a time, beating well after each addition. Set aside.
• In a small bowl, combine sour cream and milk, stirring to blend. Add vanilla extract. Set aside.
• In a medium bowl, combine flour, baking powder, and salt, whisking well. Add flour mixture to butter mixture in thirds, alternately with sour cream mixture, beginning and ending with flour mixture. Reduce mixer speed to low, and add coconut and pecans, beating until just combined.
• Using a levered 3-tablespoon scoop, divide batter among prepared wells of muffin pans.
• Bake until cupcakes are golden brown and a wooden pick inserted in the centers comes out clean, 16 to 18 minutes. Let cool slightly in pans. When cupcakes are cool enough to handle, transfer to a wire rack, and let cool completely.
• Place Italian Cream Cheese Frosting in a piping bag fitted with a large open-star tip (Wilton #1). Pipe frosting onto cooled cupcakes in a decorative swirl.
• Garnish with pecans, if desired.
• Refrigerate cupcakes, covered, until serving time.

An easy way to finely chop coconut is to pulse it in the work bowl of a food processor. Pulse first, then measure coconut.

Italian Cream Cheese Frosting

Yield: 3 cups | Preparation: 15 minutes

½ cup salted butter, softened
1 (8-ounce) package cream cheese, softened
4¼ cups confectioners' sugar
1 teaspoon vanilla extract
⅛ teaspoon salt

• In a large mixing bowl, combine butter and cream cheese. Beat at high speed with an electric mixer until creamy. Add confectioners' sugar, vanilla extract, and salt. Beginning at low speed and gradually increasing to high speed, beat until frosting is light and fluffy.

Make-Ahead Tip: *Frosting can be made a day in advance and refrigerated in a covered container until needed. Before using, beat at high speed with an electric mixer until softened and spreadable, approximately 1 minute.*

The Victorian Parlor

living the dream

The first time people visit a tearoom, they often come away vowing to open their own one day. Not everyone follows through with that dream, but Paula Senft of Spring Grove, Pennsylvania, must be the exception. She stepped inside a tearoom for the first time in 1996 and loved it so much that she came away with a bee in her bonnet (though in her case, it was probably a cute little fascinator). She convinced her husband, Daryl, that they should open one of their own. Fifteen years and three houses later, these self-admitted "people persons" are happily humming along in the historic Georgian-style Greek Revival that is home to The Victorian Parlor—and to the Senfts themselves.

Paula does all the cooking, with occasional help from the manager, and Daryl is the designated "tea man," who not only orders but also pours the blends they serve. They can seat 60-plus patrons in the main dining room and the Peacock Room (named for the striking stained-glass panel on display in the space) combined. Paula, who is quick to confess that she loves to shop, has filled the tearoom with exquisite furnishings that heighten the whole experience, although the sumptuous six-course menu is draw enough. Soup is served in big bowls, scones are always hot out of the oven, and her cakes are, in Daryl's words, "works of art." There is no set weekly or monthly menu. Paula loves to change it up, and her customers love to be surprised.

"We're definitely not stuffy," Paula says with a twinkle in her eye. And the adorable fascinator, perched jauntily on her head, confirms it.

Cocoa–Cottage Cheese Cake

Yield: 24 servings | Preparation: 30 minutes
Bake: 30 to 38 minutes

2⅔ cups sifted all-purpose flour
⅓ cup natural unsweetened cocoa powder
1 teaspoon salt
1 teaspoon baking soda
½ teaspoon baking powder
1 cup salted butter, softened
1 cup sugar
1 cup firmly packed light brown sugar
2 large eggs
¾ cup small-curd cottage cheese
1¼ cups whole buttermilk
1 cup nuts (optional)
1 recipe Sweetened Whipped Cream (recipe on page 52)
Garnish: strawberry slices

• Preheat oven to 350°.
• Lightly spray a (13-x-9-inch) cake pan with nonstick baking spray with flour. Set aside.
• In a large bowl, combine flour, cocoa powder, salt, baking soda, and baking powder, whisking well. Set aside.
• In a large mixing bowl, beat butter at medium speed with an electric mixer until creamy. Gradually add sugar and brown sugar, beating until light and fluffy. Add eggs, beating well. Add cottage cheese, beating until incorporated.
• Add flour mixture to butter mixture in thirds, alternately with buttermilk, beginning and ending with flour mixture. Add nuts (if using), stirring at low speed to combine. Spread batter into prepared pan.
• Bake until a wooden pick inserted in the center comes out clean, 30 to 38 minutes. Let cool completely in pan on a wire rack.
• Cut cake into 24 squares, trimming edges if desired.
• Just before serving, place Sweetened Whipped Cream in a piping bag fitted with a large open-star tip (Wilton #1M). Pipe a decorative swirl of whipped cream onto each cake sqaure.
• Garnish each serving with a strawberry slice, if desired.

Triple-Layer Pumpkin Cakes

Yield: 12 servings | Preparation: 45 minutes
Bake: 13 to 14 minutes | Cool: 1 hour
Freeze: 1 hour

½ cup salted butter, softened
1¼ cups firmly packed light brown sugar
2 large eggs
1 cup canned pumpkin purée
1½ teaspoons vanilla extract
2 cups sifted cake flour, such as Swans Down
1 teaspoon ground cinnamon
½ teaspoon baking powder
½ teaspoon baking soda
½ teaspoon salt
½ teaspoon ground ginger
¼ teaspoon ground nutmeg
½ cup whole buttermilk
1 recipe Orange–Cream Cheese Frosting
   (recipe follows)

• Preheat oven to 350°.
• Spray an 18-x-13-inch rimmed baking sheet with nonstick cooking spray. Line with parchment paper, and spray again. Set aside.
• In a large mixing bowl, beat butter at medium-high speed with an electric mixer until creamy. Add brown sugar, and beat until light and fluffy, approximately 3 minutes. Add eggs, one at a time, beating well after each addition. Add pumpkin purée and vanilla extract, beating until incorporated. Set aside.
• In a medium bowl, combine flour, cinnamon, baking powder, baking soda, salt, ginger, and nutmeg, whisking well. Add flour mixture to butter mixture in thirds, alternately with buttermilk, beginning and ending with flour mixture. Spread batter into prepared pan, rapping sharply on countertop to reduce air bubbles.
• Bake until a wooden pick inserted in the center comes out clean, 13 to 14 minutes. Let cool completely in pan on a wire rack.
• Remove cake from pan, and place on a cutting board. Cut cake into 3 (13-x-6-inch) portions. Using an offset spatula, spread one-fourth of Orange–Cream Cheese Frosting on 1 portion of cake. Top with another portion of cake, and spread one-third of remaining frosting on top. Top with remaining portion of cake, and spread with half of remaining frosting. Freeze assembled cake until it is firm enough to cut into cake fingers, approximately 1 hour.

• Trim rough edges from all sides of cake. Using a long, sharp knife, cut cake evenly into 12 pieces, pressing downward with knife to create a clean cut. Place cake pieces on a serving platter.
• Place remaining frosting in a pastry bag fitted with a closed-star tip (Ateco #30). Pipe frosting shells in rows on tops of cake pieces.
• Let come to room temperature before serving.

Make-Ahead Tip: Cake can be baked, frosted, and assembled a week in advance. Wrap securely in plastic wrap, and freeze until needed. Cut cake into fingers while frozen. Let thaw before piping frosting shells on top.

Kitchen Tip: To create even layers of frosting, measure equal amounts to spread between layers.

Orange–Cream Cheese Frosting

Yield: 5 cups | Preparation: 10 minutes

11 ounces cream cheese, softened
¾ cup salted butter, softened
7 cups confectioners' sugar
2 teaspoons vanilla extract
1 tablespoon fresh orange zest

• In a large mixing bowl, beat cream cheese and butter at high speed with an electric mixer until smooth and creamy. Add confectioners' sugar and vanilla extract, beating until incorporated. Beat frosting at high speed until light and fluffy. Add orange zest, beating to combine.

Make-Ahead Tip: Orange–Cream Cheese Frosting can be made a day in advance and refrigerated, covered, until needed.

"Come, let us have some tea and continue to talk about happy things."

— Chaim Potok, *The Chosen*

Chocolate-Chai Cake Bites

Yield: 15 cake bites | Preparation: 20 minutes
Bake: 11 to 12 minutes | Cool: 20 minutes

½ cup sugar
¼ cup natural unsweetened cocoa powder
1 tablespoon finely ground white cornmeal
1 teaspoon ground ginger
½ teaspoon ground Vietnamese cinnamon
½ teaspoon ground cardamom
¼ teaspoon ground cloves
⅛ teaspoon salt
2 large eggs, lightly beaten
¼ cup salted butter, melted
1¼ teaspoons vanilla extract
1 recipe Sweetened Whipped Cream (see recipe
   on page 52)
Garnish: grated chocolate

• Preheat oven to 325°.
• Spray 15 wells of a 24-well, shallow mini muffin pan*
with nonstick cooking spray. Set aside.
• In a large bowl, combine sugar, cocoa powder, cornmeal, ginger, cinnamon, cardamom, cloves, and salt,
whisking well. Set aside.
• In a medium bowl, combine eggs, melted butter, and
vanilla extract, whisking well. Add to cocoa mixture,
whisking until incorporated. Fill prepared wells of pan
approximately three-quarters full (approximately
1 tablespoon batter per well).
• Bake until puffed, 11 to 12 minutes. (Surface will look
slightly dry but will still be moist in center.) Let cool in
pan for 5 minutes. Carefully transfer to a wire rack, and
let cool completely.
• Place Sweetened Whipped Cream in a piping bag
fitted with an open-star tip (Ateco #848). Pipe cream
onto cooled cake bites.
• Garnish with grated chocolate, if desired.
• Serve immediately.

*We used a Chicago Metallic mini muffin pan with shallow
wells (approximately ¾ inch in depth), which is available at
chicagometallicbakeware.com.*

Strawberry-Ginger Roulade *(photo on page 43)*

Yield: approximately 14 servings | Preparation: 1½ hours
Bake: 6 minutes | Cool: 30 minutes

3 tablespoons fresh orange juice
1 cup plus 3 tablespoons sugar, divided
3 cups thinly sliced strawberries
4 large eggs, separated
1½ teaspoons vanilla extract, divided

¾ cup sifted cake flour, such as Swans Down
¾ teaspoon baking powder
½ teaspoon salt
¼ cup finely chopped crystallized ginger
Confectioners' sugar
2 cups heavy whipping cream
Garnish: additional confectioners' sugar and
   fresh strawberries

• Preheat oven to 375°.
• Spray 2 (9-inch) square cake pans with nonstick
cooking spray. Line pans with parchment paper.
Spray again. Set aside.
• In a medium bowl, combine orange juice and
3 tablespoons sugar, stirring until sugar dissolves.
Add strawberries, tossing to coat. Let stand at room
temperature for 1 hour.
• Meanwhile, in a mixing bowl, beat egg yolks at
medium speed with an electric mixer until light in
color, 2 to 3 minutes. Add ¾ cup sugar and 1 teaspoon
vanilla extract, beating until incorporated, 1 to 2
minutes. Set aside.
• In a medium bowl, combine flour, baking powder,
and salt, whisking well. Gradually add flour mixture
to egg mixture, beating until smooth. Set aside.
• In a separate bowl, beat egg whites at high speed
with an electric mixer until stiff peaks form. Gently fold
egg whites and ginger into batter. Divide batter evenly
between prepared pans.
• Bake until layers are light golden brown and a
wooden pick inserted in the centers comes out clean,
approximately 6 minutes.
• While cakes are baking, sift confectioners' sugar
over 2 clean thin dish towels in 9-inch squares.
• When cakes are done, immediately turn out onto
prepared dish towels. Remove parchment paper, and
roll up each cake jelly-roll style in dish towel, setting
each one seam side down on wire racks to cool.
• In a large mixing bowl, combine cream, remaining
¼ cup sugar, and remaining ½ teaspoon vanilla extract.
Beat at medium-high speed with an electric mixer until
stiff peaks form. Add enough liquid from strawberry
mixture to tint cream pink, stirring gently.
• Gently unroll cakes, and spread each with half of
whipped-cream mixture. Place half of sliced strawberries in a single layer over each whipped-cream layer.
Reroll cakes jelly-roll style, placing seam side down.
Cover, and refrigerate for up to 1 day until ready to
serve.
• Just before serving, garnish each roulade with a dusting of confectioners' sugar, if desired. Using a serrated
knife, trim ends of roulades to even. Slice roulades into
1-inch pieces.
• Garnish with fresh strawberries, if desired.

STRAWBERRY-GINGER ROULADE
(recipe on page 41)

Earl Grey–Chocolate Cake

Yield: 24 servings | Preparation: 20 minutes
Bake: 28 to 30 minutes | Cool: 1 hour

½ cup water
3 (.2-ounce) bags Earl Grey black tea
2½ cups sifted cake flour, such as Swans Down
1½ cups sugar
¾ cup unsweetened dark cocoa powder, such as
   Hershey's Special Dark
2 teaspoons baking soda
1 teaspoon salt
½ cup plus 2 tablespoons salted butter, softened
2 large eggs
2 teaspoons vanilla extract
1 cup whole buttermilk
1 recipe Dark Chocolate Ganache (recipe follows)
Garnish: Wilton Cookies & Crème Crunch Sprinkles
   and dark chocolate shards

• Preheat oven to 350°.
• Spray a 13-x-9-inch baking pan with nonstick cooking
spray. Set aside.
• In a small saucepan, heat water to boiling. Remove
from heat, and add tea bags. Cover, and let steep for
5 minutes. Remove and discard tea bags. Let tea cool
to room temperature. Set aside.
• In a large mixing bowl, combine flour, sugar, cocoa
powder, baking soda, and salt, whisking well. Add butter, eggs, vanilla extract, buttermilk, and tea. Beat at
medium speed with an electric mixer for 3 minutes.
• Pour batter into prepared baking pan, and spread
evenly.
• Bake until a wooden pick inserted in the center
comes out clean, 28 to 30 minutes. Let cool in pan on
a wire rack for 10 minutes. Invert onto a wire rack, and
let cool completely.
• Using a long, serrated knife, trim top of cake to
create a level surface, if necessary. Cut cake into 24
(2-inch) squares.
• Place cake squares on a wire rack, and spoon warm
Dark Chocolate Ganache over each square, letting
ganache drip down sides. Smooth ganache with an
offset spatula to cover cake squares, if necessary.
• Garnish with sprinkles and dark chocolate shards,
if desired.

Dark Chocolate Ganache

Yield: 3 cups | Preparation: 25 minutes

2 cups heavy whipping cream
6 (.2-ounce) bags Earl Grey black tea
1 (10-ounce) package bittersweet chocolate morsels,
   such as Ghirardelli

• In a small saucepan, heat cream until hot but not boiling. Remove from heat, and add tea bags. Cover, and
let steep for 15 minutes. Remove and discard tea bags.
Reheat cream until hot but not boiling. Remove from
heat, and add chocolate morsels, stirring until chocolate
is melted and smooth. Use immediately.

Shakespeare's Corner Shoppe & Afternoon Tea

authentically british

If you are looking for a British tea experience on the West Coast, look no further than Shakespeare's Corner Shoppe & Afternoon Tea in San Diego, California. The tea fare is as authentic as owner Selina Stockley can make it, but the "Afternoon Tea" part of the shop does have a unique West Coast vibe. Tea is served outside on an awning-covered deck so guests can enjoy the Southern California sunshine along with their scones, tea sandwiches, and cups of Earl Grey.

Selina, a native of Surrey, England, set out to see the world at age 21 and ended up falling in love with (and settling in) San Diego. She guarantees her guests a true British tea experience: "We are traditionalists and purists here. We import our double Devon cream and our jams from Britain," she says. Everything else on Shakespeare's Corner's tea tray—including Grandmother Lucy's recipe for Toffee Tea Cakes—is made from scratch by the tearoom's full-time baker and her assistant.

The other half of Shakespeare's Corner is set up like a British corner grocery store. Selina specializes in offering British expatriates in the San Diego area, as well as American fans, British products that cannot be purchased in the United States. That includes British tea brands such as Twinings and PG Tips and the shop's own line of loose-leaf teas.

"People come in for the tearoom, and then they realize we have other things that are quite nice that they might want to try," Selina explains. "It's great. People get to learn about different British foods."

Toffee Tea Cakes

Yield: 66 tea cakes | *Preparation: 30 minutes*
Bake: 14 minutes

2 cups self-rising flour
1 cup firmly packed light brown sugar
½ cup superfine or castor sugar
1 cup whole buttermilk
½ cup salted butter, melted
2 large eggs
1 teaspoon vanilla extract
¾ cup toffee chips, such as Bits 'o Brickle, divided
¼ cup finely chopped walnuts

• Preheat oven to 325°.
• Line 66 wells of 3 (24-well) mini muffin pans with paper liners. Set aside.
• In a large bowl, combine flour, brown sugar, and castor sugar, whisking to blend. Set aside.
• In another large bowl, combine buttermilk, melted butter, eggs, and vanilla extract, whisking well. Add to flour mixture, stirring until just combined. Add ½ cup toffee chips, folding to combine.
• Using a levered 2-teaspoon scoop, divide batter among prepared wells of muffin pans. Set aside.
• In a small bowl, combine remaining ¼ cup toffee chips and walnuts. Sprinkle generously and evenly over batter in each prepared well.
• Bake until light brown, approximately 14 minutes. (Turn muffin pans halfway through baking.) Remove from oven, and serve warm.

Tarts
&
Cheesecakes

LEMON, WHITE CHOCOLATE &
MASCARPONE FLOWER TARTLETS
(recipe on page 59)

Brownie Tart

Yield: 8 to 10 servings | Preparation: 20 minutes
Bake: 23 minutes | Cool: 1 hour

½ cup salted butter
4 tablespoons natural unsweetened cocoa powder
1 cup sugar
½ cup all-purpose flour
1 teaspoon baking powder
¼ teaspoon salt
2 large eggs
1 teaspoon vanilla extract
1 cup chopped, toasted pecans
Garnish: confectioners' sugar and strawberries

• Preheat oven to 350°.
• Spray a 9-inch round tart pan with a removable bottom with nonstick baking spray with flour. Sprinkle additional flour along the seam of removable bottom to prevent batter from leaking. Set aside.
• In a medium saucepan, melt butter over low heat. Add cocoa powder, stirring until smooth and creamy. Remove pan from heat, and set aside.
• In a medium bowl, combine sugar, flour, baking powder, and salt, whisking well. Add eggs and vanilla extract to butter mixture. Add flour mixture, stirring until ingredients are thoroughly blended. Add pecans, stirring to combine. Spread batter evenly in prepared tart pan.
• Bake until a wooden pick inserted in the center comes out with only a few crumbs clinging to it, approximately 23 minutes. Let tart cool completely before removing from pan.
• Garnish by sifting confectioners' sugar over top of tart and arranging strawberries in the center, if desired.

Kitchen Tip: Tart can be made in a 9-inch pie pan, and pieces cut and served from pan.

Make-Ahead Tip: Tart can be made in advance, cooled completely, wrapped securely in plastic wrap, placed in an airtight container, and frozen for up to a week. Let thaw completely before garnishing.

Key Lime Mini Cheesecakes

Yield: 12 mini cheesecakes | Preparation: 30 minutes
Bake: 16 to 17 minutes | Cool: 1 hour | Refrigerate: 4 hours

¾ cup graham cracker crumbs
⅓ cup plus 1 tablespoon sugar, divided
3 tablespoons salted butter, melted
1 (8-ounce) package cream cheese, softened
2 tablespoons bottled Key lime juice, such as Nellie and Joe's Famous Key West Lime Juice

3 teaspoons all-purpose flour
1 teaspoon fresh lime zest
1 large egg
Garnish: fresh lime slices

• Preheat oven to 350°.
• Lightly spray a 12-well mini cheesecake pan with nonstick cooking spray. Set aside.
• In a small bowl, combine graham cracker crumbs, 1 tablespoon sugar, and melted butter, stirring to blend. Divide crumb mixture evenly among wells of prepared pan, pressing firmly to create a level base.
• Bake until golden brown, approximately 6 minutes. Let cool completely.
• In a medium mixing bowl, combine cream cheese, remaining ⅓ cup sugar, lime juice, flour, and lime zest. Beat at high speed with an electric mixer until smooth and creamy. With mixer running at medium speed, add egg, beating until incorporated. Divide mixture evenly among wells of prepared pan.
• Bake until filling is set and slightly puffed, approximately 11 minutes. Let cool completely. (Cheesecakes will fall as they cool.) Refrigerate for at least 4 hours.
• Remove cheesecakes from pan.
• Garnish each with a lime slice before serving, if desired.

Make-Ahead Tip: Cheesecakes can be made a day in advance and refrigerated (ungarnished) in an airtight container. Garnish before serving. Or freeze (ungarnished) in an airtight container for up to a week. Let thaw completely before garnishing.

strawberry halves in a circle with tips pointing toward center of tartlets and propping on center strawberry. Cut reserved strawberries in half. Top each tartlet with a strawberry half.
• Garnish strawberries with a light coating of melted jelly, if desired.

Make-Ahead Tip: *Tartlet shells and filling can be made earlier in the day. Assemble tartlets up to 2 hours before serving. Refrigerate, covered, until serving time.*

Chocolate Chess Tartlets

Yield: 16 tartlets | Preparation: 45 minutes
Refrigerate: 30 minutes | Bake: 8 to 10 minutes
Cool: 1 hour

1 (14.1-ounce) package refrigerated pie dough
  (2 sheets)
2 large eggs, lightly beaten
½ cup semisweet chocolate morsels, melted
⅓ cup sugar
4 tablespoons salted butter, melted
1 tablespoon finely ground white cornmeal
1¼ teaspoons vanilla extract
⅛ teaspoon salt
1 recipe Sweetened Whipped Cream (recipe follows)
Garnish: mini chocolate curls

• Preheat oven to 450°.
• Lightly spray 16 (2½-inch) round tartlet pans with nonstick cooking spray. Place on a rimmed baking sheet, and set aside.
• On a lightly floured surface, unroll both sheets of pie dough. Using a 3-inch round cutter, cut 16 circles from dough. Press dough circles into prepared tartlet pans, as illustrated on page 129. Using a fork, prick bottoms of dough. Refrigerate for 30 minutes.
• Bake until light golden brown, 5 to 6 minutes. Let tartlet shells cool completely on baking sheet.
• In a medium bowl, combine eggs, melted chocolate, sugar, melted butter, cornmeal, vanilla extract, and salt, whisking to blend. Divide chocolate mixture among cooled tartlet shells, filling each three-quarters full.
• Bake until mixture is set and slightly puffed, 8 to 10 minutes. Let tartlets cool completely before removing from tartlet pans. (As tartlets cool, slight cracks will form in surface.)
• Place Sweetened Whipped Cream in a piping bag fitted with a large open-star tip (Wilton #1). Pipe a whipped cream rosette onto each tartlet.
• Garnish with chocolate curls, if desired.

Kitchen Tip: *To make mini chocolate curls, grate a chocolate bar, using a citrus zester.*

Strawberry-Mascarpone Tartlets

Yield: 8 tartlets | Preparation: 45 minutes
Refrigerate: 2½ hours | Bake: 7 minutes | Cool: 15 minutes

1 (8-ounce) container mascarpone cheese, softened
½ cup strawberry preserves
¼ teaspoon vanilla extract
1 pinch salt
1 (14.1-ounce) package refrigerated pie dough
  (2 sheets)
4 cups whole strawberries
Garnish: melted strawberry jelly

• In a small bowl, combine mascarpone cheese, strawberry preserves, vanilla extract, and salt, stirring to blend. Cover and refrigerate for 2 hours.
• Preheat oven to 450°.
• On a lightly floured surface, unroll both sheets of pie dough. Using a 4-inch round cutter, cut circles from pie dough. Press into 8 (4-inch) round tartlet pans with removable bottoms, as illustrated on page 129. Using a fork, prick bottoms of dough. Place prepared tartlet pans on 2 rimmed baking sheets. Refrigerate for 30 minutes.
• Bake until light golden brown, 6 to 7 minutes. Let cool completely on baking sheets.
• Divide mascarpone mixture evenly among cooled tartlet shells, smoothing to create a level surface.
• Reserve 4 strawberries for tops of tartlets. Hull remaining strawberries and cut in half. Place 1 strawberry half in center of each tartlet. Arrange remaining

Sweetened Whipped Cream
Yield: 1 cup | Preparation: 5 minutes

½ cup cold heavy whipping cream
1 tablespoon confectioners' sugar
¼ teaspoon vanilla extract

• In a small bowl, combine cream, confectioners' sugar, and vanilla extract. Beat at high speed with an electric mixer until thickened and creamy.
• Refrigerate in an airtight container until needed.

*HOW-TO
on page 127

Peach-Ginger Tartlets

Yield: 6 tartlets | Preparation: 45 minutes
Bake: 8 minutes | Cool: 30 minutes | Freeze: 2 hours

40 vanilla-wafer cookies
3 tablespoons sugar
5 tablespoons salted butter, melted
1 (8-ounce) package cream cheese, softened
3 tablespoons honey
1 tablespoon heavy whipping cream
1 teaspoon ground ginger
1 (29-ounce) can peach halves in heavy syrup

• Preheat oven to 350°.
• In the work bowl of a food processor, process cookies until finely ground.
• In a medium bowl, combine cookie crumbs, sugar, and melted butter, stirring to blend. Divide evenly among 6 (4-inch) tartlet pans with removable bottoms, pressing crumb mixture firmly into bottom and up sides of pans.
• Bake until golden brown, approximately 8 minutes. Let cool completely. Freeze to harden shells, approximately 2 hours. (This will prevent breakage when assembling tartlets.)
• In a medium mixing bowl, combine cream cheese, honey, cream, and ginger. Beat at high speed with an electric mixer until smooth and creamy.
• Reserving syrup, lay peach halves on a cutting board, rounded side up. Using a paring knife, cut peach halves into thin vertical slices, approximately ¼ inch thick. Set aside.
• Remove tartlet shells from pans. Divide cream cheese mixture among frozen tartlet shells, spreading in an even layer.
• Beginning with longest slices, build a flower shape with peaches, overlapping ends of slices.*
• Brush tartlets with reserved syrup. Serve immediately, or refrigerate, lightly covered, for up to an hour before serving.

Lemon-Chamomile Tartlets

Yield: 48 tartlets | Preparation: 30 minutes
Bake: 15 to 17 minutes

2 boxes mini (1.75-inch) shortbread tartlet shells, such as Clearbrook Farms
6 tablespoons heavy whipping cream
3 bags chamomile-citrus tea, such as Mighty Leaf
2 large eggs
½ cup sugar
2 teaspoons fresh lemon zest
¼ cup fresh lemon juice
1 recipe Meringue Topping (recipe follows)

• Preheat oven to 325°.
• Place tartlet shells on 2 rimmed baking sheets. Set aside.
• Heat cream to very hot but not boiling. Remove from heat, add tea bags, and let steep for 15 minutes. Discard tea bags. Let cool.
• In a medium bowl, combine eggs, sugar, lemon zest, lemon juice, and cooled cream, whisking to blend. Transfer mixture to a large measuring cup with a pouring spout for ease of filling tartlet shells. (Keep mixture whisked so that it does not settle.) Fill tartlet shells to just below rim.
• Bake until filling is set, approximately 10 minutes. Remove tartlets from oven.
• Increase oven temperature to 350°.
• Place Meringue Topping in a piping bag fitted with a large open-star tip (Wilton #1). Pipe a decorative swirl on top of warm tartlets.
• Return tartlets to oven, and bake until Meringue Topping is golden brown, 5 to 7 minutes.
• Serve immediately, or refrigerate until needed.

Meringue Topping

Yield: 2 cups | Preparation: 5 minutes

2 egg whites, at room temperature
3 tablespoons sugar
¼ teaspoon cream of tartar

• In a mixing bowl, combine egg whites, sugar, and cream of tartar. Beat at high speed with an electric mixer until stiff peaks form. Use immediately.

• Drop jam by tablespoonfuls onto cheesecake mixture. Drag the tip of a knife through jam and filling to create a swirled pattern.
• Bake until cheesecake is mostly firm with only a slight jiggle in the center, approximately 35 minutes. Remove to a wire rack, and let cool completely in pan.
• Freeze, covered, for at least 4 hours and up to 1 day.
• Lift cheesecake from pan, using parchment paper overhang as handles. Place on a cutting board. Cut into 16 squares.
• Store in an airtight container in the refrigerator for up to 3 days. Serve cold.

Peppermint Mini Cheesecakes

Yield: 12 mini cheesecakes | Preparation: 30 minutes
Bake: 16 to 17 minutes | Cool: 1 hour | Refrigerate: 4 hours

¾ cup graham cracker crumbs
¼ cup plus 1 tablespoon sugar, divided
3 tablespoons salted butter, melted
1 (8-ounce) package cream cheese, softened
3 teaspoons all-purpose flour
½ teaspoon vanilla extract
1 large egg
¼ cup peppermint baking chips, such as
    Andes Peppermint Crunch Baking Chips
1 recipe Sweetened Whipped Cream
    (recipe on page 52)
Garnish: peppermint candy

• Preheat oven to 350°.
• Lightly spray a 12-well mini cheesecake pan with nonstick cooking spray. Set aside.
• In a small bowl, combine graham cracker crumbs, 1 tablespoon sugar, and melted butter, stirring to blend. Divide crumb mixture evenly among wells of prepared pan, pressing to create a level base.
• Bake until golden brown, approximately 6 minutes. Let cool completely.
• In a medium bowl, combine cream cheese, remaining ¼ cup sugar, flour, and vanilla extract. Beat at high speed with an electric mixer until smooth and creamy. With mixer running at medium speed, add egg, beating until incorporated. Add peppermint baking chips, stirring to combine. Divide mixture evenly among wells of prepared pan.
• Bake until filling is set and slightly puffed, 10 to 11 minutes. Let cool completely. (Cheesecakes will fall as they cool.) Refrigerate, covered, for at least 4 hours.
• Remove cheesecakes from pan.
• Place Sweetened Whipped Cream in a piping bag fitted with a large open-star tip (Wilton #1). Pipe a whipped-cream rosette onto each cheesecake.
• Garnish each with peppermint candies, if desired.

Strawberry Cheesecake Squares

Yield: 16 servings | Preparation: 30 minutes
Bake: 50 minutes | Cool: 1 hour | Freeze: 4 hours

½ cup salted butter, softened
¾ cup sugar, divided
1½ cups plus 1 tablespoon all-purpose flour, divided
⅛ teaspoon salt
2 (8-ounce) packages cream cheese, softened
1 teaspoon fresh lemon zest
1 tablespoon fresh lemon juice
2 large eggs
½ cup strawberry jam

• Preheat oven to 350°.
• Line an 8-inch square pan with a double thickness of parchment paper, letting parchment paper hang over sides at least 1 inch. Set aside.
• In a medium mixing bowl, combine butter and ¼ cup sugar. Beat at high speed with an electric mixer until light and creamy. Add 1½ cups flour and salt, beating at low speed until combined. (Mixture will have the consistency of cornmeal.) Using hands, press mixture into bottom of prepared pan, building up a ½-inch edge on all sides.
• Bake until very light golden brown, approximately 15 minutes. Set aside to cool.
• In another medium mixing bowl, combine cream cheese, remaining ½ cup sugar, remaining 1 tablespoon flour, lemon zest, and lemon juice. Beat at medium speed until mixture is smooth, approximately 1 minute. Add eggs, beating to incorporate. Spread cheesecake mixture evenly over baked crust.

Make-Ahead Tip: Cheesecakes can be made a day in advance and refrigerated (ungarnished) in an airtight container. Garnish before serving. Or freeze (ungarnished) in an airtight container for up to 1 week. Let thaw completely before garnishing.

Swan House Tea Room
a gathering place for women

Giving something a try before you buy it is sound advice. At least it was for Bev Robb of Findlay, Ohio, when she came to work for the Swan House Tea Room more than 10 years ago. The mother of five whose children had flown the nest was looking for something to fill her time. "I was a server at the Swan House for a couple of years before I bought into the tearoom eight years ago," she recalls. "I'm really glad I did." That experience gave her a chance to learn the business before she bought out her partners in 2009.

It was while working at the Swan House that Bev developed a love of tea. "I have to have my teatime every day now," she insists. "And I love hospitality—that's my passion. Owning a tearoom is just a fun thing to do." The Swan House fills a need in rural Findlay, located in the northwest corner of Ohio, approximately 45 miles south of Toledo and Lake Erie. Although men do come to the tearoom, it's more a place where women come together.

"As I get older, I realize that women need to go where we can be pampered," she explains, "someplace that makes us feel good and makes us feel special." The Swan House provides that respite by offering both lunch and tea, Tuesday through Saturday, with a menu that changes every month and 26 varieties of tea. "We offer foods you wouldn't make at home," Bev says, "and give women a chance to relax and let someone else serve them for a change."

Pear Tartlets

Yield: 12 tartlets | *Preparation: 25 minutes*
Bake: 13 to 15 minutes | *Cool: 1 hour*
Refrigerate: 2 hours

12 (3.15-inch) shortbread tartlet shells, such
    as Clearbrook Farms
1 (8-ounce) package cream cheese, softened
¼ cup plus 1 tablespoon sugar, divided
1 large egg
1 teaspoon vanilla extract
1 (29-ounce) can pear halves, drained and
    thinly sliced
1 teaspoon ground cinnamon

• Preheat oven to 350°.
• Place tartlet shells on a rimmed baking sheet. Set aside.
• In a large bowl, beat cream cheese at high speed with an electric mixer until smooth. Add ¼ cup sugar, egg, and vanilla extract, beating to combine. Divide filling evenly among tartlet shells. Arrange 3 pear slices on each tartlet. Set aside.
• In a small bowl, combine remaining 1 tablespoon sugar and cinnamon. Sprinkle mixture over pear slices.
• Bake until filling is set and an instant-read thermometer inserted in the center of tartlets registers 160°, 13 to 15 minutes. Let tartlets cool at room temperature for 1 hour.
• Refrigerate tartlets for 2 hours before serving.

Swan House Tearoom | *225 W. Sandusky Street • Findlay, Ohio* | *419-429-7926* | *facebook.com/swanhousetearoom*

- Bake until light golden brown, 6 to 7 minutes. Let cool completely on baking sheet.
- In a medium nonstick sauté pan, combine pineapple, ½ cup sugar, egg yolks, cornstarch, lemon juice, and salt, stirring to blend. Cook over medium heat, stirring until thickened. Add butter, stirring until melted and incorporated. Remove from heat, and let cool slightly. Add coconut and macadamia nuts. Spoon mixture into cooled tartlet shells. Set aside.
- Reduce oven temperature to 375°.
- In a medium bowl, combine egg whites, remaining 2 tablespoons sugar, and cream of tartar. Beat at high speed with an electric mixer until stiff peaks form. Divide meringue evenly among tartlets, swirling with a spoon to create peaks.
- Bake until peaks of meringue are golden brown, approximately 8 minutes. Let cool slightly, and remove tartlets from tartlet pans.
- Serve at room temperature, or refrigerate, covered, for 4 hours and serve cold.

Make-Ahead Tip: *Tartlets can be made earlier in the day and refrigerated, lightly covered, until serving time.*

Pineapple, Coconut & Macadamia Custard Tartlets

Yield: 6 tartlets | Preparation: 45 minutes
Refrigerate: 4½ hours | Bake: 14 to 15 minutes
Cook: 3 to 4 minutes

1 (14.1-ounce) package refrigerated pie dough
   (2 sheets)
1 (8-ounce) can crushed pineapple, undrained
½ cup plus 2 tablespoons sugar, divided
2 large eggs, separated
1 tablespoon cornstarch
1 tablespoon fresh lemon juice
⅛ teaspoon salt
1 tablespoon salted butter
¼ cup toasted sweetened flaked coconut
¼ cup chopped macadamia nuts
¼ teaspoon cream of tartar

- Preheat oven to 450°.
- On a lightly floured surface, unroll both sheets of pie dough on a lightly floured surface. Using a 4½-inch round cutter, cut 6 circles from pie dough. Press dough circles into 6 (4-inch) round tartlet pans with removable bottoms, as illustrated on page 129. Using a fork, prick bottoms of dough. Place prepared tartlet pans on a rimmed baking sheet. Refrigerate for 30 minutes.

Lemon, White Chocolate & Mascarpone Flower Tartlets

Yield: 16 tartlets | Preparation: 30 minutes
Refrigerate: 2 hours | Bake: 7 minutes | Cool: 30 minutes

1 cup salted butter, softened
1 cup sugar
1 large egg
1 tablespoon whole milk
1 teaspoon vanilla extract
3 cups all-purpose flour
¾ teaspoon baking powder
¼ teaspoon salt
Confectioners' sugar
1 recipe Lemon–White Chocolate Mousse
   (recipe follows)
Garnish: fresh raspberries and fresh mint

- In a large bowl, combine butter and sugar. Beat at medium speed with an electric mixer until creamy. Add egg, milk, and vanilla extract, beating to combine. Set aside.
- In a medium bowl, combine flour, baking powder, and salt. Gradually add flour mixture to butter mixture, beating well to combine. Divide dough in half, and wrap each half tightly in plastic wrap. Refrigerate for 2 hours.
- Preheat oven to 375°.
- Spray 2 (12-well) whoopee pie pans with nonstick baking spray with flour. Set aside.
- On a lightly floured surface, roll each portion of

dough to a ¼-inch thickness. Using a 3½-inch flower-shaped cutter dipped in flour, cut out 16 shapes from dough. Place in wells of prepared pan. Using a fork, prick bottoms of dough.
• Bake until edges are lightly browned, approximately 7 minutes. Let cool in pans for 10 minutes. Remove tartlet shells from pan, and let cool completely on wire racks.
• Lightly sift confectioners' sugar over tops and bottoms of tartlet shells.
• Place Lemon–White Chocolate Mousse in a piping bag fitted with a large open-star tip (Wilton #1). Pipe mousse rosettes into each tartlet shell.
• Garnish with raspberries and mint, if desired.
• Serve immediately.

Lemon–White Chocolate Mousse
Yield: 4 cups | *Preparation: 10 minutes*
Refrigerate: 1 hour

2 (10-ounce) jars lemon curd, such a Dickinson's
2 (8-ounce) containers mascarpone cheese
2 (4-ounce) bars white chocolate, such as Ghirardelli, melted

• In a large bowl, whisk lemon curd vigorously to loosen. Add mascarpone cheese, whisking until incorporated. Add melted white chocolate, whisking to blend.
• Refrigerate in a covered container for at least 1 hour until needed.

Sweet Potato Tartlets

Yield: 6 tartlets | Preparation: 30 minutes
Bake: 30 to 35 minutes | Cool: 30 minutes

3 cups cubed raw sweet potatoes
1 (14.1-ounce) package refrigerated pie dough
   (2 sheets)
2 tablespoons salted butter, melted
¼ cup sugar
2 tablespoons heavy whipping cream
2 tablespoons whole milk
¾ teaspoon vanilla extract
¼ teaspoon ground cinnamon
⅛ teaspoon ground nutmeg
⅛ teaspoon salt
1 large egg
1 recipe Sweetened Whipped Cream
   (recipe on page 52)
Garnish: ground nutmeg

• Preheat oven to 350°.
• Place sweet potatoes in a medium saucepan with
enough water to cover. Bring to a boil over medium
heat. Cover, and cook until tender, approximately 15
minutes. Drain sweet potatoes, and let cool. Using a
potato masher, mash sweet potatoes. (You should have
approximately 1½ cups.) Set aside.
• On a lightly floured surface, unroll both sheets of
pie dough. Using a 4½-inch round cutter, cut 6 circles
from pie dough. Press into 6 (4-inch) tartlet pans with
removable bottoms, as illustrated on page 129. Place
prepared pans on a rimmed baking sheet. Set aside.
• In a large mixing bowl, combine sweet potatoes,
melted butter, sugar, cream, milk, vanilla extract, cinnamon, nutmeg, and salt. Beat at medium speed with
an electric mixer until smooth. Add egg, beating well.
Divide mixture evenly among prepared tartlet shells.
• Bake until filling is set and a knife inserted in the
centers comes out clean, 30 to 35 minutes. Let cool
completely before removing tartlets from pans.
• Place Sweetened Whipped Cream in a piping bag
fitted with a small closed-star tip (Ateco #30). Pipe
rosettes onto surfaces of tartlets.
• Garnish each with a dusting of ground nutmeg, if
desired.
• Serve at room temperature, or refrigerate, covered,
until needed, and serve cold.

Chocolate–Peanut Butter Tartlets

Yield: 24 tartlets | Preparation: 25 minutes
Microwave: 1½ minutes | Refrigerate: 30 minutes

½ cup peanut butter morsels
1 cup plus 2 tablespoons heavy whipping cream, divided

2 tablespoons creamy peanut butter
1 (4-ounce) bar bittersweet chocolate, such as
   Ghirardelli, finely chopped
1 box mini (1.75-inch) shortbread tartlet shells,
   such as Clearbrook Farms
2 tablespoons confectioners' sugar
½ teaspoon vanilla extract
Garnish: mini dark chocolate curls

• In a medium microwave-safe bowl, combine peanut
butter morsels and 2 tablespoons cream. Microwave at
50 percent power for 15-second intervals until melted,
approximately 1½ minutes. Stir until smooth. Add peanut butter, stirring until combined. Let cool slightly.
• In a small saucepan, heat ½ cup cream almost to
boiling. Remove from heat, and add chocolate. Let
mixture stand for 1 minute. Stir until smooth.
• Place tartlet shells on a small tray. Divide chocolate
mixture evenly among tartlet shells. Refrigerate until
chocolate is firm, approximately 30 minutes.
• In a small bowl, combine remaining ½ cup cream,
confectioners' sugar, and vanilla extract. Beat at medium
speed with an electric mixer until thick, stopping just before stiff peaks form. Add cream mixture to cooled peanut
butter mixture, whisking well.
• Transfer mixture to a piping bag fitted with a large
open-star tip (Wilton #1). Pipe onto tartlets.
• Garnish with chocolate curls, if desired.

Kitchen Tip: *To make mini chocolate curls, grate a
chocolate bar, using a citrus zester.*

Make-Ahead Tip: *Tartlets can be made earlier in the
day and refrigerated (without peanut butter whipped
cream) in an airtight container. Let come to room temperature before garnishing and serving.*

Gorgonzola-Pear Tartlets

Yield: 4 tartlets | *Preparation: 20 minutes*
Refrigerate: 30 minutes | *Bake: 15 minutes*
Cool: 15 minutes

½ (14.1-ounce) package refrigerated pie dough
  (1 sheet)
3 ripe Bartlett pears
1 tablespoon fresh lemon juice
2 tablespoons salted butter
2 tablespoons all-purpose flour
2 tablespoons sugar
⅛ teaspoon salt
¼ cup crumbled Gorgonzola cheese
Garnish: honey and chopped toasted almonds

• Preheat oven to 450°.
• On a lightly floured surface, unroll pie dough. Using a 4½-inch round cutter, cut 4 circles from pie dough. Press dough circles into 4 (4-inch) round tartlet pans, as illustrated on page 129. Place pans on a rimmed baking sheet. Using a fork, prick bottoms of dough. Refrigerate for 30 minutes.
• Bake until light golden brown, approximately 5 minutes. Let cool completely, and remove from tartlet pans.
• Peel pears, and dice into ½-inch cubes. Toss lightly with lemon juice. Divide pears evenly among prebaked tartlet shells. Set aside.
• In a small bowl, combine butter, flour, sugar, and salt, rubbing between fingers to form a thick paste. Divide butter mixture among tartlets, scattering randomly over pears. Sprinkle cheese over tartlets, dividing evenly.
• Bake until pears are soft and cheese is lightly browned, approximately 10 minutes.

• Garnish with a drizzle of honey and chopped toasted almonds, if desired.
• For best results, make and serve the same day.

Kitchen tip: *If pie dough starts to puff during baking, prick it again with a fork.*

Blueberry-Lemon Mini Cheesecakes

Yield: 12 mini cheesecakes | *Preparation: 30 minutes*
Bake: 17 to 20 minutes | *Cool: 15 minutes*
Refrigerate: 4 hours

¾ cup graham cracker crumbs
⅓ cup plus 1 tablespoon sugar, divided
3 tablespoons salted butter, melted
1 (8-ounce) package cream cheese, softened
3 teaspoons all-purpose flour
1 teaspoon fresh lemon zest
2 tablespoons fresh lemon juice
1 large egg
Garnish: fresh blueberries and fresh mint

• Preheat oven to 350°.
• Lightly spray a 12-well mini cheesecake pan with nonstick cooking spray. Set aside.
• In a small bowl, combine graham cracker crumbs, 1 tablespoon sugar, and melted butter, stirring to blend. Divide crumb mixture evenly among wells of prepared pan, pressing firmly to create a level base.
• Bake until golden brown, approximately 6 minutes. Let cool completely.
• In a medium bowl, combine cream cheese, remaining ⅓ cup sugar, flour, lemon zest, and lemon juice. Beat at medium speed with an electric mixer until smooth and creamy. With mixer running at medium speed, add egg, beating until incorporated. Divide mixture evenly among wells of prepared pan.
• Bake until filling is set and slightly puffed, approximately 11 minutes. Let cool completely. (Cheesecakes will fall as they cool.) Refrigerate, covered, for at least 4 hours.
• Remove cheesecakes from pan.
• Garnish with blueberries* and mint before serving, if desired.

*For additional sweetness, toss blueberries in simple syrup, if desired.

Make-Ahead Tip: *Cheesecakes can be made a day in advance and refrigerated (ungarnished) in an airtight container. Garnish before serving. Or freeze (ungarnished) in an airtight container for up to 1 week. Let thaw completely before garnishing.*

Make-Ahead Tip: Jam Puffs can be made earlier in the day, placed in an airtight container, and refrigerated until serving time. Garnish with confectioners' sugar just before serving.

Jam Puffs

Yield: 12 pastries | Preparation: 25 minutes
Bake: 10 minutes | Cool: 30 minutes

1 (17.3-ounce) box frozen puff pastry sheets
1 (3-ounce) package cream cheese, softened
1 tablespoon confectioners' sugar
¼ teaspoon vanilla extract
1 large egg
1 tablespoon water
¼ cup assorted fruit preserves*
Garnish: confectioners' sugar

• Preheat oven to 400°.
• Line a rimmed baking sheet with parchment paper. Set aside.
• Let puff pastry sheets thaw just until they can be unfolded and smoothed flat. (This will make them easier to cut and assemble). Using a 1½-inch square cutter, cut 36 squares from pastry sheets. Using a 1-inch round cutter, cut centers from 24 squares.
• Stack 2 squares with centers cut out on top of a solid square, aligning edges to form a perfect square, and place on prepared baking sheet. Repeat with remaining squares. Cover with plastic wrap to prevent drying out while mixing filling.
• In a small bowl, combine cream cheese, confectioners' sugar, and vanilla extract. Beat at medium speed with an electric mixer until blended. Transfer cream-cheese mixture to a piping bag fitted with medium round tip (Wilton #12). (If a piping bag is not available, use a resealable plastic bag with a corner snipped off.) Pipe a small button of cream cheese mixture into each puff-pastry cavity.
• In a small bowl, combine egg and water, whisking to blend. Lightly brush mixture over tops of puff pastry.
• Bake until pastries have risen and are golden brown, 8 to 10 minutes. Remove from oven, and fill each pastry with ¼ teaspoon of your favorite fruit preserves. Let cool completely.
• Garnish with a dusting of confectioners' sugar just before serving, if desired.

We used peach preserves, blueberry preserves, strawberry preserves, and red currant jelly.

Pistachio-Orange Tartlets

Yield: 12 tartlets | Preparation: 45 minutes
Refrigerate: 30 minutes | Bake: 18 to 20 minutes
Cool: 1 hour

1 (14.1-ounce) package refrigerated pie dough (2 sheets)
1 large egg
½ cup firmly packed light brown sugar

3 tablespoons light corn syrup
1 tablespoon salted butter, melted
1 teaspoon vanilla extract
1 teaspoon fresh orange zest
½ cup plus 2 tablespoons finely chopped roasted, salted pistachios
Garnish: fresh orange zest curls

• Preheat oven to 450°.
• Lightly spray 12 (4-x-2¼-inch) diamond-shaped tartlet pans with nonstick cooking spray. Set aside.
• On a lightly floured surface, unroll both sheets of pie dough. Using a tartlet pan as a guide, cut 12 shapes from pie dough. Press dough shapes into prepared tartlet pans, as illustrated on page 129. Using a fork, prick bottoms of dough. Place prepared tartlet pans on a rimmed baking sheet. Refrigerate for 30 minutes.
• Bake until very light golden brown, 5 to 7 minutes. Let cool completely on baking sheet.
• Reduce oven temperature to 350°.
• In a medium bowl, combine egg, brown sugar, corn syrup, melted butter, vanilla extract, and orange zest, whisking to blend. Add pistachios, stirring to combine. Divide mixture evenly among cooled tartlet shells, filling each three-quarters full.
• Bake until filling is set and slightly puffed, approximately 13 minutes. Let cool completely in pans. Remove tartlets from pans.
• Garnish each with an orange zest curl, if desired.

Kitchen tip: *Pistachios in the shell tend to be a brighter green than shelled pistachios. To give these tartlets their best color, we recommend buying pistachios in the shell and shelling your own.*

Kitchen Tip: *For this recipe, we recommend that you make the Brown Sugar Glaze first since 1 tablespoon of it is added to the tartlet filling.*

Bananas Foster Tartlets

Yield: 4 tartlets | *Preparation: 30 minutes*
Cook: 2 to 3 minutes | *Refrigerate: 8 hours*
Bake: 7 to 8 minutes | *Cool: 30 minutes*

½ cup plus 2 tablespoons canned coconut milk
¼ cup sugar
1 tablespoon all-purpose flour
⅛ teaspoon salt
¼ teaspoon vanilla extract
1 recipe Brown Sugar Glaze (recipe follows)
½ (14.1-ounce) package refrigerated pie dough (1 sheet)
1 to 2 bananas, cut into ¼-inch slices

• In a small saucepan, combine coconut milk, sugar, flour, and salt. Cook over medium-high heat, whisking constantly, until mixture just comes to a boil. Remove from heat, and add vanilla extract, stirring to blend. Let cool slightly, whisking occasionally.
• Add 1 tablespoon Brown Sugar Glaze to custard, whisking well. Place a sheet of plastic wrap on surface of custard. Refrigerate until cold, 8 hours or overnight.
• On a lightly floured surface, unroll pie dough. Using a 4½-inch round cutter, cut 4 circles from dough. Press circles into 4 (4-inch) round tartlet pans with removable bottoms, as illustrated on page 129. Using a fork, prick bottoms of dough. Place prepared tartlet pans on a

rimmed baking sheet. Refrigerate for 30 minutes.
• Preheat oven to 450°.
• Bake until golden brown, 7 to 8 minutes. Let tartlet shells cool completely before removing from tartlet pans.
• Evenly divide cooled custard among baked tartlet shells. Arrange banana slices on top of custard in concentric circles, overlapping banana slices slightly. Brush Brown Sugar Glaze over bananas. Serve immediately.

Brown Sugar Glaze
Yield: ¼ cup | Preparation: 10 minutes | Cook: 2 to 3 minutes

1 tablespoon salted butter
¼ cup firmly packed light brown sugar
1 tablespoon plus 2 teaspoons dark rum
⅛ teaspoon ground cinnamon

• In a small saucepan, melt butter over low heat. Add brown sugar, rum, and cinnamon, whisking until sugar melts and ingredients are blended.
• Reserving 1 tablespoon glaze for tartlet filling, cover and refrigerate remaining glaze until needed.
• In a sauté pan, gently warm Brown Sugar Glaze over low heat, whisking glaze as it melts until smooth.

Decadent Chocolate Mini Cheesecakes
Yield: 12 mini cheesecakes | Preparation: 30 minutes
Bake: 16 to 17 minutes | Cool: 1 hour
Refrigerate: 4 hours

¾ cup chocolate wafer crumbs, such as Nabisco
   Famous Chocolate Wafers
¼ cup plus 1 tablespoon sugar, divided
3 tablespoons salted butter, melted
1 (8-ounce) package cream cheese, softened
3 teaspoons all-purpose flour
½ teaspoon vanilla extract
1 egg
1 (4-ounce) bittersweet chocolate bar, such as
   Ghirardelli, melted
1 recipe Semisweet Ganache (recipe follows)
Garnish: fresh raspberries and fresh mint

• Preheat oven to 350°.
• Lightly spray a 12-well, square mini cheesecake pan with nonstick cooking spray. Set aside.
• In a small bowl, combine chocolate wafer crumbs, 1 tablespoon sugar, and melted butter, stirring to blend. Divide crumb mixture evenly among wells of prepared pan, pressing firmly to create a level base.
• Bake until set, approximately 6 minutes. Let cool completely.

• In a medium bowl, combine cream cheese, remaining ¼ cup sugar, flour, and vanilla extract. Beat at high speed with an electric mixer until smooth and creamy. With mixer running on medium speed, add egg, beating until incorporated. Add melted chocolate, beating until incorporated. Divide mixture evenly among wells of prepared pan.
• Bake until cheesecakes are set and slightly puffed, 10 to 11 minutes. Let cool completely. Refrigerate, covered, for at least 4 hours.
• Remove cheesecakes from pan just before serving. Spread Semisweet Ganache onto cheesecakes.
• Garnish with raspberries and mint, if desired.

Make-Ahead Tip: *Cheesecakes can be made a day in advance and refrigerated (ungarnished, without raspberries and mint) in an airtight container. Garnish before serving. Or freeze (ungarnished) in an airtight container for up to a week. Let thaw completely before garnishing.*

Semisweet Ganache
Yield: ⅓ cup | Preparation: 10 minutes

¼ cup heavy whipping cream
½ cup semisweet chocolate morsels

• In a small saucepan, heat cream over medium-high heat until very hot with bubbles forming around edges of pan. Remove from heat, and add chocolate morsels. Stir until chocolate is melted and mixture is smooth and creamy.

Cookies
& Bars

BONBON COOKIES
(recipe on page 97)

Chocolate-Dipped Peanut Butter Cookies

Yield: 44 cookies | Preparation: 30 minutes
Bake: 8 minutes | Cool: 2½ hours

1 cup creamy peanut butter
1 cup sugar
1 teaspoon vanilla extract
1 large egg
2 cups semisweet chocolate morsels
Garnish: finely chopped salted peanuts

• Preheat oven to 350°.
• Line 2 rimmed baking sheets with parchment paper. Set aside.
• In a medium bowl, combine peanut butter, sugar, vanilla extract, and egg. Beat at medium speed with an electric mixer until ingredients are incorporated.
• Using a levered 1-teaspoon scoop, divide dough into portions, and place 2 inches apart on prepared baking sheets. Using the bottom of a glass dipped in additional sugar, flatten cookies.
• Bake until cookies are puffed and set, approximately 8 minutes. Let cool on baking sheets for 1 to 2 minutes. Transfer to wire cooling racks, and let cool completely.
• In a small bowl, melt chocolate morsels according to package directions. Dip 1 end of cookies into melted chocolate, and place on a wire cooling rack.
• While chocolate is still wet, garnish with chopped peanuts, if desired. Let cool until chocolate is firm, approximately 2 hours.
• Store in between layers of waxed paper in an airtight container at room temperature for 2 to 3 days.

Fig Crumb Bars

Yield: 32 bars | Preparation: 30 minutes
Cook: 13 minutes | Bake: 32 minutes

1 cup chopped dried figs
1 cup water
¾ cup plus 2 tablespoons quick-cooking oats
¾ cup plus 2 tablespoons all-purpose flour
½ cup firmly packed light brown sugar
½ teaspoon baking soda
½ cup cold salted butter
½ cup sugar
1 tablespoon plus ¼ teaspoon cornstarch
¼ teaspoon ground cinnamon
2 large egg yolks
¾ cup sour cream
1 teaspoon vanilla extract

• Preheat oven to 350°.
• Line an 8-inch square baking pan with a double thickness of parchment paper, letting edges of parchment paper hang over edges of pan. Spray with nonstick cooking spray. Set aside.
• In a small saucepan, combine figs and water. Bring to a boil, then reduce heat so that figs simmer slightly. Cook for 10 minutes. Drain figs well, and discard water. Set figs aside.
• In a medium bowl, combine oats, flour, brown sugar, and baking soda, whisking well. Using a pastry blender, cut butter into oat mixture until crumbly. Continue to work mixture with hands, rubbing butter into oat mixture until mixture is uniformly moist. Press half of oat mixture into bottom of prepared pan, creating a level base. Reserve remaining half.
• Bake until light golden brown, approximately 7 minutes. Set aside to cool.
• In a small saucepan, combine sugar, cornstarch, and cinnamon, whisking well. Add egg yolks, sour cream, and vanilla extract, whisking until incorporated. Cook over low heat until thickened and creamy (similar to pudding), approximately 3 minutes. Add figs, stirring to combine. Pour mixture into cooled crust. Crumble remaining half of oat mixture evenly over filling.
• Bake until set and golden brown, approximately 25 minutes. Let cool completely before cutting. Lift bars from pan, using parchment paper as handles. Cut into 2-x-1-inch bars.
• Serve at room temperature, or refrigerate overnight and serve cold.

Make-Ahead Tip: *Make and bake bars a day in advance, cover, and refrigerate. Cut into bars while cold, and serve immediately or let come to room temperature.*

Ginger-Almond Cookies

Yield: approximately 35 cookies | Preparation: 15 minutes
Bake: 5 minutes per batch

2 large egg whites
½ cup sugar
⅓ cup all-purpose flour
2 tablespoons minced crystallized ginger
3 tablespoons salted butter, melted and cooled
¼ cup sliced almonds

• Preheat oven to 400°.
• In a medium mixing bowl, beat egg whites at high speed with an electric mixer until stiff peaks form. Sprinkle sugar over egg whites, and fold in, using a spatula. Add flour and crystallized ginger, folding to combine. Add melted butter, folding to incorporate. Set aside.
• Coat a baking sheet with butter and flour. Place prepared baking sheet in oven for 5 minutes.
• Drop batter by teaspoonfuls onto hot baking sheet. Working quickly and using an offset spatula, spread batter for each cookie thinly to silver-dollar size. Sprinkle cookies with almonds.
• Bake until cookies are light brown around edges, approximately 3 minutes.
• Let cool briefly, approximately 1 minute, on baking sheet. Transfer to a wire rack, and let cool completely. (Cookies should have a crispy yet chewy texture.) Repeat baking-sheet preparation and procedure for remaining batches of cookies.
• Store at room temperature in an airtight container.

Greek Easter Cookies (Koulourakia)

Yield: 58 cookies | Preparation: 30 minutes
Bake: 10 to 11 minutes

1 cup salted butter, softened
1½ cups sugar
3 large eggs
½ teaspoon vanilla extract
¼ teaspoon almond extract
¼ teaspoon anise extract
1 tablespoon fresh orange zest
½ cup fresh orange juice
6 cups all-purpose flour
2 teaspoons baking powder
½ teaspoon baking soda
1 large egg, beaten
½ cup whole milk
3 tablespoons sesame seeds

• Preheat oven to 375°.
• Line several rimmed baking sheets with parchment paper. Set aside.
• In a large mixing bowl, combine butter and sugar. Beat at high speed with an electric mixer until light and fluffy, approximately 1 minute. Add eggs, one at a time, beating thoroughly after each addition. Add extracts, orange zest, and orange juice, beating to combine. (Mixture will appear curdled.) Set aside.
• In a large bowl, combine flour, baking powder, and baking soda, whisking well. Add flour mixture to butter mixture in thirds. (Dough will be soft but not sticky.)
• Using a levered 1½-tablespoon scoop, divide dough into portions. On a lightly floured surface and using hands, roll portions into 6-x-½-inch ropes. Fold each dough rope in half, and twist to form a braid.* Place 2 inches apart on prepared baking sheets. Set aside.
• In a small bowl, combine egg and milk, whisking well. Brush cookies with egg mixture, and sprinkle with sesame seeds.
• Bake until edges of cookies are light golden brown, approximately 10 minutes. Transfer to wire racks, and let cool completely.
• Store at room temperature in airtight containers to maintain cookies' soft breadlike texture.

Make-Ahead Tip: *Cookies can be baked in advance, placed in airtight containers, with layers separated by waxed paper, and frozen for up to 2 weeks. Let cookies thaw before serving.*

*HOW-TO on page 126

Pickwick Society Tea Room
an endless pot of kindness

Anyone who has read the classic novel *Little Women* will remember the tea parties and amateur theatricals the March sisters, Meg, Jo, Beth, and Amy, held in the attic of their family home, Orchard House. They called these impromptu gatherings the Pickwick Society after the novel by British author Charles Dickens.

When Heidi Vassell opened a tearoom in Frankfort, Illinois, in 2004, she thought the name fit the casual theme of her new business, so she named it the Pickwick Society Tea Room. Just the year before, Heidi had graduated from college with three degrees—all in the arts. "Art history, museum studies, and French," recalls her mother, Cindy Vassell. "Her job prospects were not looking good."

Cindy owned an antiques store in the heart of Frankfort's historic district, and her daughter noticed that a retail space across the street was for lease. "It was a quaint Cape Cod cottage, the perfect place for a tearoom," Cindy says. Before she knew it, Heidi had talked to the landlord, written a business plan, and applied for a business license. "She came to me and said, 'I'm going to be your neighbor now.'"

Although Heidi has since moved out of state, the Pickwick Society Tea Room continues in the way she wanted—tea is accessible to everybody. Cindy, who manages the tearoom for her daughter, explains, "It's a very casual tearoom. We don't have a dress code." And the *Little Women* theme is carried throughout. "All our menus are named for the March girls," she says, including a Marmee's Full Tea. "That comes with an endless pot of tea because Marmee had endless kindness."

Blueberry–White Tea Shortbread
Yield: 100 cookies | Preparation: 25 minutes
Bake: 8 to 10 minutes | Refrigerate: 30 minutes

1 cup sugar
4 tablespoons blueberry white tea leaves, such as Octavia Tea Company Wild Blueberry Organic White Tea
1 teaspoon salt
2 cups salted butter, softened
2 teaspoons water
2 teaspoons vanilla extract
4 cups all-purpose flour
1 cup confectioners' sugar
½ cup chopped dried blueberries (optional)

• Line several rimmed baking sheets with parchment paper.
• In the work bowl of a food processor, combine sugar, tea leaves, and salt. Pulse until tea leaves are pulverized. Set aside.
• In a large mixing bowl, combine butter, water, and vanilla extract. Beat at medium speed with an electric mixer until blended. Add pulverized tea mixture, stirring to combine. Add flour and confectioners' sugar, beating at medium speed just until dough is smooth. Fold in dried blueberries, if desired.
• Divide dough into 4 equal portions, and shape into logs with square sides. Wrap each log in plastic wrap, and refrigerate for at least 30 minutes or overnight.
• Preheat a convection oven to 325° (350° for a conventional oven).
• Cut cookies into ¼-inch slices, and place 1 inch apart on prepared baking sheets.
• Bake until cookies are set and light brown around edges, 8 to 10 minutes. Let cool on baking sheet for 1 to 2 minutes. Transfer to a wire rack, and let cool completely.
• Store cookies in an airtight container at room temperature for up to 1 week.

Pickwick Society Tea Room | *122 W. Kansas Street* | *Frankfort, Illinois 60423* | *815-806-8140* | pickwicktearoom.com

Triple-Layer Brownies

Yield: 64 brownies | Preparation: 30 minutes
Microwave: 2 to 3 minutes | Bake: 30 to 33 minutes
Cool: 15 minutes | Refrigerate: 2 to 4 hours

2½ cups dark chocolate morsels, such as Ghirardelli,
   divided
¾ cup salted butter, softened and divided
1¼ cups sugar
3 large eggs
1½ teaspoons vanilla extract, divided
1 cup all-purpose flour
¾ teaspoon salt, divided
1 cup creamy peanut butter
¾ cup confectioners' sugar
1 tablespoon whole milk
½ cup heavy whipping cream

• Preheat oven to 350°.
• Line a 9-inch square baking pan with heavy-duty foil.
Spray foil with nonstick cooking spray. Set aside.
• In a large microwave-safe bowl, combine 1½ cups
chocolate morsels and ½ cup butter. Microwave for
1-minute intervals at 50 percent power, stirring to
combine, until mixture is smooth.
• Add sugar, stirring to combine. Add eggs, one at a
time, stirring well after each addition. Add ½ teaspoon
vanilla extract, stirring well. Set aside.
• In a small bowl, combine flour and ½ teaspoon salt,
whisking well. Add to chocolate mixture, stirring to
incorporate. Pour batter into prepared pan.
• Bake until a wooden pick inserted in the center
comes out clean, 30 to 33 minutes. Let cool until
slightly warm, approximately 15 minutes.

• In a medium bowl, combine peanut butter, remaining ¼ cup butter, confectioners' sugar, remaining
¼ teaspoon salt, milk, and remaining 1 teaspoon
vanilla extract, stirring until blended.
• While brownie layer is slightly warm, use an offset
spatula to spread peanut butter mixture over top in
a smooth layer. Set aside.
• In a small saucepan, heat cream until almost boiling.
Remove from heat, and add remaining 1 cup chocolate
morsels, stirring until smooth. Pour over peanut butter
layer, spreading into a smooth layer. Refrigerate until
chocolate layer becomes firm, 2 to 4 hours.
• Using edges of foil as handles, lift whole brownie
from pan. Carefully remove foil, and place brownie on
a cutting board. Using a long chef's knife, score chocolate ganache into 1-inch squares. To cut into individual
brownies, line up knife with scored lines, pressing
down firmly in one motion.
• Refrigerate, covered, for up to 3 days.

Strawberry French Madeleines

Yield: 48 madeleines | Preparation: 20 minutes
Bake: 5 minutes

1 cup all-purpose flour
1 teaspoon baking powder
⅛ teaspoon salt
4 large eggs
¾ cup sugar
2 teaspoons strawberry extract
½ cup salted butter, melted and cooled
Garnish: confectioners' sugar

• Preheat oven to 350°.
• Spray 4 (12-well) madeleine pans with nonstick baking spray with flour. Set aside.
• In a small bowl, combine flour, baking powder, and
salt. Set aside.
• In a large mixing bowl, combine eggs, sugar, and
strawberry extract. Beat at high speed with an electric
mixer until pale and fluffy, approximately 5 minutes.
Gradually add half of flour mixture to egg mixture,
beating at medium speed until incorporated. Slowly
add butter, beating until well blended. Add remaining
flour mixture, beating until incorporated. Let batter
stand for 5 minutes.
• Spoon 1 tablespoon batter into each prepared pan,
smoothing with fingertip to create a level surface.
• Bake until light golden, approximately 5 minutes.
Remove madeleines from molds, and let cool
completely on wire racks.
• Dust with confectioners' sugar, if desired.

Make-Ahead Tip:
Strawberry French
Madeleines can be
made ahead and fro-
zen (ungarnished) in an
airtight container for
up to 1 week. Let thaw
before dusting with
confectioners' sugar.

Lemon-Lavender Shortbread

Yield: approximately 34 cookies | *Preparation: 20 minutes*
Bake: 50 minutes | *Cool: 1 hour*

1 cup salted butter, softened
¼ cup firmly packed light brown sugar
½ cup confectioners' sugar
1 tablespoon fresh lemon zest
1½ teaspoons lemon extract
2 cups all-purpose flour
1 teaspoon dried culinary lavender
¼ teaspoon salt

• Preheat oven to 300°.
• Line an 8-inch square baking pan with a double thickness of parchment paper, letting paper hang over sides. Spray with nonstick cooking spray. Set aside.
• In a large mixing bowl, combine butter, brown sugar, confectioners' sugar, lemon zest, and lemon extract. Beat at medium-high speed with an electric mixer until light and creamy, 2 to 3 minutes. Set aside.
• In a medium bowl, combine flour, lavender, and salt, whisking well. Add to butter mixture, beating until incorporated. Press dough evenly into prepared pan*.
• Bake until shortbread is light golden brown, approximately 50 minutes. Place pan on a wire rack, and let cool completely.
• When cool, lift shortbread from pan, using parchment paper overhang as handles, and place on a cutting surface. Using a long, sharp knife, cut by pressing down to create clean cuts.
• Store in an airtight container until serving time.

Make-Ahead Tip: *Lemon-Lavender Shortbread can be baked in advance and frozen in an airtight container for up to 2 weeks.*

*To prevent sticking, use latex gloves or lightly dampen hands with water while pressing.

Lemon-Pistachio Shortbread

Yield: 36 (1¼-inch) squares | *Preparation: 20 minutes*
Bake: 50 minutes

1 cup plus 1 teaspoon salted butter, softened
   and divided
¼ cup firmly packed light brown sugar
½ cup confectioners' sugar
1 tablespoon fresh lemon zest
½ teaspoon lemon extract
2 cups all-purpose flour
¼ teaspoon salt
¼ cup finely chopped, roasted pistachios, divided

• Preheat oven to 300°.
• Butter an 8-inch square baking pan with 1 teaspoon butter. Set aside.
• In a large mixing bowl, combine remaining 1 cup butter, brown sugar, confectioners' sugar, lemon zest, and lemon extract. Beat at high speed with an electric mixer until light and creamy, 2 to 3 minutes.
• In a medium bowl, combine flour and salt, whisking well. Add to butter mixture, beating until incorporated.
• Reserve 2 teaspoons chopped pistachios, and add remainder to dough, stirring well.
• Press dough evenly into prepared pan*. Using a sharp knife, lightly score 36 squares on dough. Sprinkle reserved pistachios over dough.
• Bake until shortbread is pale brown and firm, approximately 50 minutes. Let cool, then cut along scored lines.
• Store in an airtight container.

*To prevent sticking, use latex gloves or lightly dampen hands with water while pressing.

Avalon Tearoom
& Pastry Shoppe

a leap of faith

January traditionally is a time for new beginnings. It was for Ellie and Al Kilgore when they purchased the Avalon Tearoom & Pastry Shoppe this past January. "We prayed about it long and hard," Ellie recalls, "and then my husband and I decided to take a big leap of faith." The Kilgores bought the 13-year-old tearoom in White Bear Lake, Minnesota.

As anyone with a sense of geography might imagine, it gets terribly cold in Minnesota during the winter months. And this past winter was probably one of the worst in many years, Ellie says. "People were staying at home rather than venturing out in the cold to patronize restaurants." She and Al wondered if they had made a mistake by buying the Avalon. But the weather turned out to be a blessing in disguise. "It gave us time to catch our breath," Ellie says. "It was God's way of giving us time to take a look at the business and decide what changes we should make."

In addition to making physical changes, such as remodeling the kitchen, painting the dining rooms and adding more tables, Ellie has tweaked the menu and rethought the Avalon's marketing plan. "Many customers thought this was just a formal tearoom; they didn't realize that the Avalon also serves breakfast and lunch," she says. The Kilgores hope the renovations will help the tearoom draw more customers.

"White Bear Lake still has that small-town feel, and I think the Avalon Tearoom can be such an asset to the community," Ellie says. "I want to introduce people to the whole experience of having tea."

Coconut-Cranberry Bars
Yield: 24 bars | Preparation: 10 minutes
Bake: 25 to 28 minutes | Cool: 1 hour

1½ cups graham cracker crumbs
½ cup salted butter, melted
1½ cups white chocolate morsels
1½ cups dried cranberries
1 (14-ounce) can sweetened condensed milk
1 cup sweetened, flaked coconut
1 cup toasted chopped pecans

• Preheat oven to 350°.
• Lightly spray a 13-x-9-inch baking pan with cooking spray. Set aside.
• In a small bowl, combine graham cracker crumbs and melted butter. Press into bottom of prepared pan, creating a level base. Set aside.
• In a large bowl, combine white chocolate morsels, cranberries, condensed milk, coconut, and pecans. Spread over prepared crust.
• Bake for 25 to 28 minutes. Let cool completely before cutting into bars.
• Store bars in an airtight container at room temperature.

GLUTEN FREE

Matcha French Macarons

Raspberry French Macarons

Macadamia–Vanilla Bean Macarons

Kitchen Tip: To measure confectioners' sugar accurately, spoon lightly into a measuring cup, and level off, using a straight edge. Do not pack or scoop sugar into cup as this will negatively affect final product.

Macadamia–Vanilla Bean Macarons

Yield: 24 sandwich cookies | Preparation: 5 hours
Bake: 22 to 24 minutes | Cool: 15 minutes

3 large egg whites
1 cup salted whole macadamia nuts
2 cups confectioners' sugar, divided (see Kitchen
  Tip on page 83)
2 tablespoons sugar
1 vanilla bean, split lengthwise, seeds scraped
  and reserved
1 recipe White Chocolate–Lemon Ganache
  (recipe follows)

• Place egg whites in a medium mixing bowl, and let stand, uncovered, at room temperature for exactly 3 hours. (Aging the egg whites in this manner is essential to creating perfect macarons.)
• Line 2 rimmed baking sheets with parchment paper. Using a pencil, draw 1½-inch circles 2 inches apart on parchment paper. Turn parchment paper over. Set aside.
• In the work bowl of a food processor, combine macadamia nuts and 1 tablespoon confectioners' sugar, pulsing until very finely ground. (Don't overprocess or you will create a nut butter. Nut particles should stay separate and dry, not clump together.) Add remaining confectioners' sugar and reserved vanilla bean seeds, and process just until combined. Set aside.
• Beat egg whites at medium-high speed with an electric mixer until frothy. Gradually add sugar, beating at high speed until stiff peaks form, 3 to 5 minutes. (Egg whites will be thick, creamy, and shiny.) Add macadamia nut mixture to egg whites, folding gently until well combined. Let batter stand for 15 minutes.
• Transfer batter to a piping bag fitted with a medium round tip (Wilton #12). Pipe batter onto drawn circles on prepared baking sheets. Slam baking sheets vigorously on countertop 5 to 7 times to release air bubbles. Let stand at room temperature for 45 to 60 minutes before baking to help develop the macaron's signature crisp exterior when baked. (Macarons should feel dry to the touch and should not stick to finger.)
• Preheat oven to 275°.
• Bake until firm to the touch, 23 to 24 minutes. Let cool completely on pans. Transfer to airtight containers. Refrigerate until ready to fill and serve.
• Place White Chocolate–Lemon Ganache in a pastry bag fitted with a medium round tip (Wilton #12). Pipe ganache onto flat side of macaron, and top with another macaron, flat sides together. Push down lightly and twist so that filling spreads to edges. Repeat with remaining macarons and filling.
• Serve immediately, or refrigerate in an airtight container for up to 3 days. Let come to room temperature before serving.

White Chocolate–Lemon Ganache

Yield: 1 cup | Preparation: 15 minutes | Cool: 30 minutes

2 (4-ounce) white chocolate baking bars,
  such as Ghirardelli
½ cup heavy whipping cream
1 tablespoon fresh lemon zest

• Finely chop white chocolate, and place in a medium bowl. Set aside.
• In a small saucepan, heat cream over medium-high until very hot but not boiling. Pour hot cream over chocolate, and stir until chocolate melts and mixture is smooth and creamy. Add lemon zest, stirring to combine. Place bowl in a larger bowl filled with ice. Let cool, stirring frequently.

Raspberry French Macarons

Yield: 28 sandwich cookies | Preparation: 5 hours
Bake: 20 minutes | Cool: 15 minutes

3 large egg whites
¾ cup toasted slivered almonds*
2 cups confectioners' sugar
  (see Kitchen Tip on page 83)
½ cup freeze-dried raspberries, such as Just Raspberries
2 tablespoons sugar
1 recipe Cream Cheese Filling (recipe on page 85)

• Place egg whites in a medium bowl, and let stand, uncovered, at room temperature for exactly 3 hours. (Aging the egg whites in this manner is essential to creating perfect French macarons.)
• Line several baking sheets with parchment paper. Using a pencil, draw 1½-inch circles 2 inches apart on parchment paper. Turn parchment paper over. Set aside.
• In the work bowl of a food processor, combine almonds, 1 tablespoon confectioner's sugar, and raspberries, pulsing until very finely ground. (Don't overprocess, or you will create a nut butter. Nut particles should stay separate and dry but not clump together.) Add remaining confectioners' sugar, and process just until combined. Set aside.
• Beat egg whites at medium-high speed with a mixer until frothy. Gradually add sugar, beating at high speed until stiff peaks form, 3 to 5 minutes. (Egg whites will be thick, creamy, and shiny.) Add almond mixture to egg whites, folding gently by hand until well combined. Let batter stand for 15 minutes.
• Transfer batter to a pastry bag fitted with a medium round tip (Wilton #12). Pipe batter onto drawn circles on prepared baking sheets. Slam baking sheets vigorously on countertop 5 to 7 times to release air bubbles.

(Continues on page 85)

(Continued from page 84)

- Let stand at room temperature for 45 to 60 minutes before baking to help develop the macaron's signature crisp exterior when baked. (Macarons should feel dry to the touch and should not stick to finger.)
- Preheat oven to 275°.
- Bake until firm to the touch, approximately 22 minutes. Let cool completely on pans. Transfer to airtight containers. Refrigerate until ready to fill and serve.
- Place Cream Cheese Filling in a pastry bag fitted with a medium round tip (Wilton #12). Pipe filling onto flat side of macaron, and top with another macaron, flat sides together. Push down lightly and twist so that filling spreads to edges. Repeat with remaining macarons and filling.
- Serve immediately, or refrigerate in an airtight container for up to 3 days. Let come to room temperature before serving.

*For best results, we recommend using Planters Recipe Ready Slivered Almonds.

Cream Cheese Filling

Yield: 1 cup | Preparation: 5 minutes

1 (8-ounce) package cream cheese, softened
1 tablespoon heavy whipping cream
¼ teaspoon vanilla extract
⅓ cup confectioners' sugar

- In a small bowl, beat cream cheese and cream at medium speed with an electric mixer until smooth and creamy. Add vanilla extract and confectioners' sugar, beating until incorporated. Refrigerate in a covered container until needed.

Matcha French Macarons

Yield: 24 sandwich cookies | Preparation: 5 hours
Bake: 22 minutes | Cool: 15 minutes

3 large egg whites
1 cup toasted slivered almonds*
2 cups confectioners' sugar, divided
   (see Kitchen Tip on page 83)
1 tablespoon matcha powdered green tea,
   such as Harney & Sons
2 tablespoons sugar
1 recipe Strawberry-Mascarpone Filling (recipe follows)

- Place egg whites in a medium bowl, and let stand, uncovered, at room temperature for exactly 3 hours. (Aging the egg whites in this manner is essential to creating perfect French macarons.)

- Line several baking sheets with parchment paper. Using a pencil, draw 1½-inch circles 2 inches apart on parchment paper. Turn parchment paper over. Set aside.
- In the work bowl of a food processor, combine almonds, 1 tablespoon confectioners' sugar, and matcha tea, pulsing until very finely ground. (Don't overprocess, or you will create a nut butter. Nut particles should stay separate and dry but not clump together.) Add remaining confectioners' sugar, and process just until combined. Set aside.
- Beat egg whites at medium-high speed with an electric mixer until frothy. Gradually add sugar, beating at high speed until stiff peaks form, 3 to 5 minutes. (Egg whites will be thick, creamy, and shiny.) Add almond mixture to egg whites, folding gently by hand until well combined. Let batter stand for 15 minutes.
- Transfer batter to a pastry bag fitted with a medium round tip (Wilton #12). Pipe batter onto drawn circles on prepared baking sheets. Slam baking sheets vigorously on countertop 5 to 7 times to release air bubbles. Let stand at room temperature for 45 to 60 minutes before baking to help develop the macaron's signature crisp exterior when baked. (Macarons should feel dry to the touch and should not stick to finger.)
- Preheat oven to 275°.
- Bake until firm to the touch, approximately 22 minutes. Let cool completely on pans. Transfer to airtight containers. Refrigerate until ready to fill and serve.
- Place Strawberry-Mascarpone Filling in a pastry bag fitted with a medium round tip (Wilton #12). Pipe onto flat side of macaron, and top with another macaron, flat sides together. Push down lightly and twist so that filling spreads to edges. Repeat with remaining macarons and filling.
- Serve immediately, or refrigerate in an airtight container for up to 3 days. Let come to room temperature before serving.

*For best results, we recommend using Planters Recipe Ready Slivered Almonds.

Strawberry-Mascarpone Filling

Yield: 1½ cups | Preparation: 5 minutes
Refrigerate: 1 hour

1 (8-ounce) container mascarpone cheese
½ cup strawberry preserves

- In a small bowl, combine mascarpone cheese and strawberry preserves, stirring until combined. Refrigerate in a covered container until cold, approximately 1 hour.

GLUTEN FREE

Kitchen Tip: To measure nuts for macarons accurately, spoon lightly into a measuring cup, and level off, using a straight edge.

Teaberry's Tea Room
following a different path

When you accept a challenge, you are never sure where it might lead. That was true for Susan Peterson, owner of Teaberry's Tea Room in Flemington, New Jersey, when she volunteered to organize a Christmas tea for her local garden club years ago.

"I'm just that kind of person," she explains. "When I get into something, I grow it." Once Susan started learning about tea, she wanted to know more about its history and traditions. "Before I knew it, other garden clubs were asking me to speak to their groups," she recalls. "Then museums and arboretums. That's what led me to open Teaberry's."

Trained as a bacteriologist, Susan had changed careers and worked in restaurants before she married. After she had children, she opened a small catering business in her home. "I love hospitality and cooking, and I've always had my hands in food," Susan says. "But never in a million years did I think I would own a restaurant." As it turned out, all her past experiences, from collecting china to speaking to garden clubs, had prepared her to open a tearoom.

Teaberry's is inside a lovingly restored Victorian mansion in Flemington, a town that grew up around the house that Samuel Fleming built in 1756 (hence, Fleming's Town, or Flemington). The building's bright cranberry-colored shutters are eye-catching and almost seem to greet customers, who may come for lunch or afternoon tea, Tuesday through Sunday.

The venue has turned into a family affair for the Peterson family. Susan's husband, Andrew, helps with the books, and her daughter, Sara, now manages the tearoom. Sara hopes to take over the tearoom for her mother some day.

Lemon-Currant Cookies
Yield: approximately 59 cookies
Preparation: 30 minutes | Bake: 15 minutes per batch
Cool: 15 minutes

½ cup unsalted butter, softened
1 cup sugar
¼ cup sour cream
1 large egg
1½ cups all-purpose flour
¼ teaspoon baking powder
¼ teaspoon salt
½ cup dried currants
1 tablespoon fresh lemon zest

• Preheat oven to 350°.
• Line several rimmed bakings sheets with parchment paper. Set aside.
• In a large bowl, beat butter at medium speed with an electric mixer until creamy. Add sugar, beating until light and fluffy. Add sour cream and egg, beating to incorporate. Set aside.
• In a separate bowl, combine flour, baking powder, and salt, whisking well. Gradually add flour mixture to butter mixture, mixing well. Add currants and zest, stirring to combine. (Dough will be very sticky.)
• Use a levered 1-teaspoon scoop, divide dough into portions. Using floured hands, roll portions into tiny balls. Place 2 inches apart on prepared baking sheets.
• Bake until a wooden pick inserted in the centers comes out clean, approximately 15 minutes per batch. Transfer to wire racks, and let cool completely.
• Store in an airtight container at room temperature.

Make-Ahead Tip: *Cookies can be baked in advance, placed in an airtight container with layers separated by waxed paper, and frozen for up to 1 week. Let thaw completely before garnishing with confectioners' sugar.*

Stenciled Gingerbread Cookies

Yield: approximately 41 cookies | Preparation: 40 minutes
Refrigerate: 1 hour | Bake: 8 minutes | Cool: 15 minutes

3 cups all-purpose flour
3 teaspoons ground cinnamon
2 teaspoons ground ginger
½ teaspoon baking soda
½ teaspoon ground cloves
½ teaspoon salt
¼ teaspoon baking powder
¼ teaspoon ground nutmeg
⅛ teaspoon ground black pepper
½ cup salted butter, softened
½ cup firmly packed light brown sugar
½ cup molasses
1 large egg
Garnish: confectioners' sugar

• Preheat oven to 350°.
• Line several rimmed baking sheets with parchment paper. Set aside.
• In a large bowl, combine flour, cinnamon, ginger, baking soda, cloves, salt, baking powder, nutmeg, and pepper, whisking well.
• In a large mixing bowl, combine butter and brown sugar. Beat at medium speed with an electric mixer until well combined. Add molasses and egg, beating until incorporated. Add flour mixture, beating until a moist dough forms. Divide dough into 2 portions, and wrap each securely in plastic wrap. Refrigerate until dough is firm enough to roll out, approximately 1 hour.
• On a lightly floured surface, roll each dough portion to an ⅛-inch thickness. Using a 3-inch round scalloped-edge cutter, cut circles from dough, and place 2 inches apart on prepared pans. Reroll scraps as necessary.
• Bake for 8 minutes. Transfer cookies to wire racks, and let cool completely.
• When ready to serve, garnish with a dusting of confectioners' sugar, using a variety of stencils*, if desired.

We used Martha Stewart Crafts stencils.

Apricot, Pistachio & Rosemary Biscotti

Yield: approximately 24 biscotti | Preparation: 35 minutes
Bake: 39 to 48 minutes | Cool: 30 minutes

⅔ cup sugar
2 large eggs
1¼ teaspoons vanilla extract
1¾ cups all-purpose flour
1 teaspoon baking powder
1 teaspoon finely chopped fresh rosemary

¼ teaspoon salt
½ cup chopped, salted, roasted pistachios
½ cup finely chopped dried apricots

• Preheat oven to 350°.
• Line 2 rimmed baking sheets with parchment paper. Set aside.
• In a large mixing bowl, combine sugar and eggs. Beat at high speed with an electric mixer until pale and fluffy, 3 to 5 minutes. Add vanilla extract, beating to blend. Set aside.
• In a medium bowl, combine flour, baking powder, rosemary, and salt, whisking well. Add flour mixture to egg mixture, beating until incorporated. Add pistachios and apricots, beating at low speed just until incorporated.
• Turn dough out onto a floured surface. Using floured hands, roll into a 14-x-2-inch log shape. Place dough log on a prepared baking sheet.
• Bake until log is light brown and a wooden pick inserted in the center comes out clean, 25 to 30 minutes. (Log may crack during baking.) Transfer to a wire rack, and let cool until able to handle.
• Reduce oven temperature to 325°.
• Transfer log to a cutting surface. With a serrated knife, cut log diagonally into ¼-inch pieces, using a sawing motion. Lay slices flat on remaining prepared baking sheet.
• Bake for 6 to 8 minutes, turn slices over, and bake until light golden brown, an additional 8 to 10 minutes. Transfer slices to wire racks, and let cool completely.
• Store in airtight containers for up to 2 weeks.

Ivy Garden Tearoom
a true people person

When most people near age 65, they begin to think about slowing down and retiring. But for Sue Gates, who turned 71 in February 2014, age is just a number. At 69, she purchased the Ivy Garden Tearoom in Albany, Oregon, 70 miles south of Portland, and so far, she says, she loves it.

Sue had owned a gift shop, For Yours, for 14 years when the tearoom next door came up for sale. "I had owned restaurants before opening For Yours, and I really enjoyed them," she recalls. "Running a tearoom was something different." She couldn't resist the opportunity to buy it.

The appeal of owning a tearoom went much further for Sue. "I really enjoy people—that's probably the biggest thing. You have to love people to be in this kind of business." She adds with a chuckle, "I just wish I were a little younger. Running a tearoom is kind of hard work."

The Ivy Garden, open for lunch and afternoon tea, offers more than 100 varieties of loose-leaf tea, freshly brewed in the pot or available in bulk packaging to take home. Almost everything Sue serves is made from scratch on the premises. Every table has a different theme. Each is adorned with beautiful linens and set with matching china—everything from teacups to teapots—that Sue decorates herself and sells next door in her gift shop.

The tearoom attracts a good mix of both local customers and tourists. "We even get people from Britain who say the Ivy Garden reminds them of an English tearoom," says Sue. Her customers hope the Ivy Garden Tearoom—and Sue—will be around for many years.

Macadamia Nut–Banana Bars

Yield: 24 bars | Preparation: 20 minutes
Bake: 22 to 25 minutes | Cool: 1 hour

½ cup salted butter, softened
2 cups sugar
3 bananas, peeled and mashed
1 teaspoon vanilla extract
2 cups all-purpose flour
1 teaspoon baking soda
1 pinch salt
1 recipe Cream Cheese Frosting (recipe follows)
¼ cup chopped macadamia nuts

- Preheat oven to 350°.
- Line a 13-x-9-inch baking pan with a double thickness of parchment paper, letting paper hang over sides of pan. Spray parchment paper lightly with nonstick cooking spray. Set aside.
- In a large mixing bowl, combine butter and sugar. Beat at medium speed with an electric mixer until light and fluffy. Add bananas and vanilla extract, beating to combine. Set aside.
- In a medium bowl, combine flour, baking soda, and salt, whisking well. Add flour mixture to banana mixture, beating at low speed to combine. Spread batter evenly into prepared pan.
- Bake until lightly browned, 22 to 25 minutes. Let cool completely in pan.
- Spread Cream Cheese Frosting over cooled banana layer. Sprinkle macadamia nuts evenly over frosting layer..
- Lift dessert from pan, using parchment paper overhang as handles. Cut into 24 squares.

Make-Ahead Tip: Macadamia Nut–Banana Bars can be made ahead and frozen (unfrosted) for up to 1 week. Let thaw before frosting and sprinkling with macadamia nuts.

Cream Cheese Frosting
Yield: 2 cups | Preparation: 10 minutes

½ cup salted butter, softened
1 (8-ounce) package cream cheese, softened
4½ cups confectioners' sugar
1 teaspoon vanilla extract

• In a large bowl, combine butter and cream cheese. Beat at medium-high speed with an electric mixer until creamy. Gradually add confectioners' sugar, beginning at low speed and gradually increasing to medium-high speed. Add vanilla extract, beating to incorporate.
• Use immediately, or refrigerate, covered, until needed.

"I am beginning to learn that it is the sweet, simple things of life which are the real ones after all."

Laura Ingalls Wilder

Orange Madeleines

Yield: 40 madeleines | Preparation: 30 minutes
Bake: 8 to 9 minutes | Cool: 15 minutes | Set: 2 hours

½ cup all-purpose flour
¼ teaspoon baking powder
⅛ teaspoon salt
1 large egg
6 tablespoons sugar
2½ teaspoons fresh orange zest, divided
¼ cup salted butter, melted and cooled
1½ cups confectioners' sugar
¼ cup fresh orange juice

• Preheat oven to 350°.
• Spray 2 (20-well) mini madeleine pans with nonstick baking spray with flour. Set aside.
• In a small bowl, combine flour, baking powder, and salt, whisking well. Set aside.
• In a large mixing bowl, combine egg, sugar, and 2 teaspoons orange zest. Beat at high speed with an electric mixer until light and fluffy, approximately 5 minutes. Gradually add flour mixture to egg mixture, beating at medium speed until incorporated. Slowly add melted butter, beating at low speed until incorporated. Let batter stand for 5 minutes.
• Spoon 1 teaspoon batter into each well of prepared pans, smoothing with fingertip to create a level surface.
• Bake until edges of madeleines are golden brown and a wooden pick inserted in the centers comes out clean, 8 to 9 minutes. Let cool in pans for 5 minutes. Transfer madeleines to a wire rack, and let cool completely.
• In a bowl, combine confectioners' sugar, orange juice, and remaining ½ teaspoon orange zest, whisking until smooth and creamy. Pour glaze over cookies, letting excess drip off. Let glaze dry on cookies until surface no longer feels wet, approximately 2 hours.
• Store in an airtight container until serving time.

Make-Ahead Tip: Cookies can be baked a week in advance and frozen, unglazed, in an airtight container. Let thaw completely before glazing.

Russian Almond Tea Cake Cookies

Yield: approximately 24 cookies | Preparation: 20 minutes
Bake: 14 minutes | Cool: 15 minutes

½ cup salted butter, softened
½ cup confectioners' sugar, divided
1 teaspoon almond extract
1 cup all-purpose flour
⅛ teaspoon salt
½ cup finely chopped blanched almonds

• Preheat oven to 325°.
• Line 2 baking sheets with parchment paper. Set aside.
• In a large mixing bowl, beat butter at medium speed with an electric mixer until smooth and creamy. Add ¼ cup confectioners' sugar and almond extract, beating until light and creamy. Add flour and salt, stirring until well combined. Add almonds, stirring well. Using a levered 2-teaspoon scoop, drop dough onto prepared baking sheets.
• Bake until cookie edges are light brown, approximately 14 minutes. Remove from cookie sheet while warm, and roll in remaining ¼ cup confectioners' sugar. Let cool on wire racks. Roll in confectioners' sugar again before serving, if desired.

The Baron's
Tea House

tea and flip-flops

When people receive an invitation to tea at a Victorian tearoom, often their first thought is, *What should I wear?* The dress code at The Baron's Tea House is a little more relaxed than one might expect. According to owner Erica Teets, it's not uncommon to welcome guests who are wearing shorts and flip-flops. That's just part and parcel of owning a tearoom in Crestview, Florida, in the Florida Panhandle, just a 45-minute drive from the white-sand beaches of the Gulf Coast.

"Being in Florida, we're very casual around here," Erica explains. Although some little girls (as well as their moms) come dressed to the nines for the full tea experience, casual dress is more common. "We encourage our guests to dress as they like and to make of the tea experience whatever they want."

Erica, who once worked for a federal contractor, discovered the ritual of taking tea while on a government project in Japan. She fell in love with Japanese tea traditions. Later, when she quit work to stay at home with her newborn daughter, she started an at-home tea-party business that brought the experience of sharing tea with friends to people in their homes. When a customer told her about a local tearoom that was for sale, Erica couldn't resist taking a look. She ended up buying the quaint board-and-batten cottage lock, stock, and tea kettle.

Erica offers one more concession to the laid-back lifestyle of the Florida Panhandle. At The Baron's Tea House, all 50 teas on the menu are available hot or iced.

Mojito Bars

Yield: 24 bars | Preparation: 30 minutes
Bake: 43 to 47 minutes | Cool: 1 hour

1 cup salted butter, melted
1 cup plus 1 tablespoon confectioners' sugar, divided
2 cups all-purpose flour, divided
⅜ teaspoon salt, divided
3 tablespoons light rum or 1½ teaspoons rum
   extract plus 3 tablespoons water
16 fresh mint leaves, chopped
4 large eggs
1½ cups sugar
2 teaspoons fresh lime zest
⅔ cup fresh lime juice (approximately 6 limes)
2 tablespoons whole milk
2 to 3 drops green food coloring, if desired

- Preheat oven to 350°.
- Line a 13-x-9-inch baking pan with a double thickness of parchment paper, letting paper hang over sides of pan. Spray lightly with nonstick cooking spray. Set aside.
- In a large mixing bowl, combine butter and 1 cup confectioners' sugar. Beat at medium speed with an electric mixer until light and creamy. Add 1¾ cups flour and ⅛ teaspoon salt, beating at low speed until combined. Press mixture into bottom of prepared pan.
- Bake until crust is set and lightly browned, 18 to 20 minutes. Let cool on a wire rack.
- In a small bowl, combine rum and mint. Set aside.
- In a large bowl, combine eggs and sugar, whisking well. Add remaining ¼ cup flour and remaining ¼ teaspoon salt, whisking until blended. Add lime zest, lime juice, milk, and food coloring.
- Place a strainer over a medium bowl, and pour rum mixture through strainer. Using the back of a spoon, press mixture to extract liquid from mint leaves; discard leaves. Add strained rum to egg mixture, whisking until well combined. Pour over baked crust.
- Bake until center of filling is set, 25 to 27 minutes. Let cool completely in pan, approximately 1 hour.
- Sprinkle with remaining 1 tablespoon confectioners' sugar. Lift dessert from pan, using parchment paper overhang as handles. Cut into 24 bars.
- Refrigerate bars in an airtight container until needed.

Bonbon Cookies

Yield: approximately 27 cookies | Preparation: 30 minutes
Bake: 11 to 12 minutes | Cool: 30 minutes

1½ cups confectioners' sugar, divided
½ cup salted butter, softened
3 tablespoons light brown sugar
1 tablespoon heavy whipping cream
3½ teaspoons vanilla extract, divided
½ teaspoon almond extract
1½ cups all-purpose flour
⅛ teaspoon salt
Toasted nuts (such as macadamias or cashews)
    or dried fruit (such as cherries or apricots)
2 tablespoons whole milk
Pink and green gel food coloring, such as
    Betty Crocker Classic Gel Food Colors

• Preheat oven to 350°.
• Line 2 baking sheets with parchment paper. Set aside.
• In a medium bowl, combine ½ cup confectioners' sugar, butter, brown sugar, cream, 2½ teaspoons vanilla extract, and almond extract, stirring until smooth. Add flour and salt, stirring until incorporated. (If dough seems dry, add more cream, 1 tablespoon at a time, until a dough forms.)
• Using a levered 1-tablespoon scoop, divide dough into portions. Press nuts or dried fruit into dough while still in scoop, then drop 1 inch apart onto prepared baking sheets, rounded side up.

• Bake until set but not brown, 11 to 12 minutes. Remove cookies from baking sheets, and let cool completely on wire racks.
• In a medium bowl, combine remaining 1 cup confectioners' sugar, milk, and remaining 1 teaspoon vanilla extract, whisking until completely smooth. Divide into 2 equal portions. Tint 1 portion with pink food coloring and the other with green food coloring. Dip tops of cookies into tinted icing. Dry, icing side up, on wire racks.
• Store at room temperature in an airtight container.

Make-Ahead Tip: Bonbon Cookies can be made in advance and frozen (unglazed) in an airtight container for up to 1 week. Let thaw before glazing.

Orange Marmalade Thumbprint Cookies

Yield: 48 cookies | Preparation: 15 minutes
Bake: 15 to 20 minutes

2¼ cups all-purpose flour
1 teaspoon baking powder
¼ teaspoon salt
1 cup salted butter, softened
⅔ cup sugar
2 large egg yolks
1 tablespoon fresh orange zest
1 tablespoon fresh orange juice
1 teaspoon vanilla extract
½ cup orange marmalade

• Preheat oven to 350°.
• Line 2 baking sheets with parchment paper. Set aside.
• In a medium bowl, combine flour, baking powder, and salt, whisking well. Set aside.
• In a large mixing bowl, combine butter and sugar. Beat at medium speed with an electric mixer until light and creamy. Add egg yolks, orange zest, orange juice, and vanilla extract, beating to combine. Add flour mixture to egg mixture in 2 portions, beating until moist clumps form. Gather dough into a ball.
• Shape dough into 1-inch balls. Place 1 inch apart on prepared baking sheets.
• Using a floured finger or a ½-teaspoon measuring spoon, make a depression in the center of each ball. Divide marmalade among depressions (½ teaspoon each).
• Bake until golden brown, 15 to 20 minutes. Transfer cookies to wire racks, and let cool completely.
• Refrigerate cookies in an airtight container.

Make-Ahead Tip: Orange Marmalade Thumbprint Cookies can be made ahead and frozen for up to 1 week. Let thaw before serving.

Key Lime Bars

Yield: 32 bars | Preparation: 30 minutes | Bake: 45 minutes

½ cup salted butter, softened
1¼ cups sugar, divided
1½ cups all-purpose flour, divided
⅛ teaspoon salt
3 large eggs
1 tablespoon fresh lime zest
⅓ cup Key lime juice, such as Nellie and Joe's Famous
   Key West Lime Juice*
Garnish: confectioners' sugar

• Preheat oven to 350°.
• Line an 8-inch square baking pan with aluminum foil, leaving a 1-inch overhang on all sides. Set aside.
• In a medium mixing bowl, combine butter and ¼ cup sugar. Beat at high speed with an electric mixer until light and creamy. Set aside.
• In a small bowl, combine 1 cup flour and salt, whisking well. Add flour mixture to butter mixture, stirring until incorporated.
• Using floured hands, press dough into the bottom of prepared baking pan, building up a ½-inch edge on all sides.
• Bake until light golden brown, approximately 15 minutes. Set aside to cool.
• In another bowl, combine eggs, remaining 1 cup sugar, lime zest, lime juice, and remaining ½ cup flour, whisking well. Pour over cooled crust.
• Bake until filling is set, approximately 30 minutes. Let cool to room temperature.
• Using aluminum foil as handles, remove dessert from pan. Trim away sides of crust, if desired. Cut dessert into 32 (2-x-1-inch) bars.
• Garnish with a dusting of confectioners' sugar, if desired.

Fresh lime juice may be substituted, but the flavor will not be as tart.

Other Sweets

COCONUT–VANILLA BEAN
PANNA COTTAS
(recipe on page 114)

*"In the sweetness of friendship let there
be laughter, and sharing of pleasures."*

— Khalil Gibran

Éclairs

Yield: 24 éclairs | Preparation: 1 hour
Bake: 15 minutes | Cool: 30 minutes

¾ cup water
6 tablespoons salted butter, cubed, at room
　temperature
2 teaspoons sugar
¼ teaspoon salt
¾ cup all-purpose flour
3 large eggs, at room temperature
1 recipe Vanilla Pastry Cream (recipe follows)
1 recipe Chocolate Glaze (recipe follows)

• Preheat oven to 400°.
• Line 2 rimmed baking sheets with silicone baking
mats or parchment paper. Set aside.
• In a medium saucepan, combine water, butter, sugar,
and salt. Cook over medium heat until butter melts.
Add flour all at once, stirring vigorously with a wooden
spoon. Cook and stir until dough pulls away from sides
of pan, 1 to 2 minutes. Remove pan from heat, and let
stand for 2 minutes, stirring a few times to cool dough.
• Add eggs, one at a time, stirring constantly and
vigorously with a wooden spoon until each egg is well
incorporated. (Dough should be smooth and shiny.)
Transfer dough to a resealable plastic bag with a corner
snipped off to make a ½-inch opening. Pipe dough
onto prepared baking sheets in 3-inch lengths, spacing
1 inch apart.
• Bake until golden brown, approximately 15 minutes.
Let cool completely before filling.
• Using a serrated knife, cut éclair shells in half lengthwise. Place Vanilla Pastry Cream in a resealable plastic
bag with a corner snipped off to make a ½-inch opening. Pipe pastry cream onto bottom halves of shells.
Top with remaining halves of éclair shells. Set aside.
• Place Chocolate Glaze in a piping bag, and snip
off tip of bag. Pipe glaze on top of éclairs.
• Serve immediately, or refrigerate for up to 2 hours
before serving.

*Make-Ahead Tip: Éclair shells can be made in advance
and frozen (unfilled) in an airtight container for up to a
week. Let thaw completely before filling.*

Vanilla Pastry Cream

Yield: 1¾ cups | Preparation: 20 minutes
Cook: 2 to 3 minutes | Refrigerate: 4 to 6 hours

4 large egg yolks
½ cup sugar
2 cups whole milk
3 tablespoons cornstarch
⅛ teaspoon salt
1 tablespoon butter
1½ teaspoons vanilla extract

• In a medium bowl, combine egg yolks and sugar,
whisking well. Set aside.
• In a medium saucepan, heat milk to very hot but
not boiling. Add hot milk, ¼ cup at a time, to eggs to
temper, whisking constantly. Add cornstarch and salt,
whisking until incorporated. Strain mixture through a
fine-mesh sieve.
• Return mixture to saucepan, and cook over medium
heat, whisking constantly until mixture thickens.
Remove from heat, and pour into a heatproof bowl.
Cover with plastic wrap, letting plastic touch surface
of custard. Refrigerate until custard is very cold, 4 to
6 hours or overnight.

Chocolate Glaze

Yield: ⅔ cup | Preparation: 15 minutes

½ cup heavy whipping cream
1 (4-ounce) bar semisweet chocolate, such as
　Ghirardelli, very finely chopped

• In a small saucepan, heat cream almost to boiling.
Remove pan from heat, and add chocolate, stirring
until chocolate melts and mixture is smooth. Let cool
slightly until somewhat thickened before using.

Bittersweet Chocolate–Apricot Truffles

Yield: 9 truffles | Preparation: 20 minutes
Freeze: 15 minutes | Refrigerate: 4 hours

½ cup heavy whipping cream
1 cup bittersweet chocolate morsels
1 teaspoon vanilla extract
3 tablespoons chopped dried apricots
1 cup finely ground chocolate wafer crumbs
¼ cup butter, melted and cooled
Garnish: additional finely ground chocolate-wafer
   crumbs and 9 matchstick-size pieces dried apricot,
   rolled into rosettes

• In a small saucepan, heat cream to scalding.
• In a medium bowl, combine hot cream and chocolate
morsels. Let stand for 2 to 3 minutes to melt chocolate,
stirring until smooth. Add vanilla extract, stirring well.
Add chopped apricots, stirring to combine.
• Divide chocolate mixture among wells of a 9-well
silicone brioche mold*. Tap mold on counter to level
mixture and release air bubbles. Place mold on a
rimmed baking sheet, and freeze for 15 minutes.
• In a small bowl, combine wafer crumbs and butter,
stirring until crumbs are uniformly moist. Divide crumb
mixture among prepared wells of mold, patting firmly
to set crumbs. Refrigerate for 4 hours.
• When ready to serve, remove from wells, and invert
so crumb base is on the bottom.
• Garnish with additional wafer crumbs and dried
apricots, if desired.

We used Gastroflex's 9-well silicone brioche mold
(pastrychef.com).

Crème Caramel

Yield: 12 (4-ounce) servings | Preparation: 20 minutes
Bake: 33 to 36 minutes | Refrigerate: 8 hours or overnight

1⅓ cups sugar, divided
1 cup heavy whipping cream
1 cup whole milk
⅛ teaspoon salt
1 vanilla bean, split lengthwise, seeds scraped
   and reserved
1 large egg
4 egg yolks
Garnish: edible flowers*

• Preheat oven to 325°.
• Place a clean dish towel in the bottom of a baking
dish large enough to accommodate 12 (4-ounce)
ovenproof ramekins. Set aside.
• In a medium sauté pan, melt 1 cup sugar over
medium-low heat, shaking pan occasionally as sugar
melts to evenly distribute color. Cook sugar until it
turns medium amber.
• Working very quickly, divide caramelized sugar mixture among ramekins, swirling and tilting each ramekin
so that caramel coats bottom. Set aside.
• In a medium saucepan, combine cream, milk, salt,
and reserved vanilla beans. Heat over medium heat
until very hot but not boiling. (Bubbles should appear
around edges of pan, and mixture should produce
steam.) Remove pan from heat. Set aside.
• In a small bowl, combine egg, egg yolks, and remaining ⅓ cup sugar, whisking well. Slowly add 1 cup hot
cream mixture to egg yolk mixture, whisking constantly
to temper eggs. Add tempered egg mixture to hot
cream mixture, whisking constantly. Transfer hot cream
mixture to a large liquid-measuring cup with a pouring
spout. Evenly divide hot cream mixture among ramekins.
• Fill baking dish with enough boiling water to come
halfway up sides of ramekins, being careful not to get
water in ramekins.
• Bake just until custard is set, approximately 33 minutes. (A very slight jiggle is OK. Custard will firm up as
it chills.) Let ramekins sit in water bath for 5 minutes.
Remove from pan, and let cool completely on wire racks.
• Place ramekins in a deep dish or pan, and wrap with
plastic wrap, but don't let wrap touch surface of
custard. Refrigerate until serving time.
• Just before serving, dip bottom half of ramekins into
boiling water for 10 seconds. Place a dessert plate over
each ramekin; invert, giving ramekin a shake until it
releases onto plate.
• Garnish with edible flowers, if desired.
• Serve immediately.

GLUTEN
FREE

*We used edible flowers from Gourmet
Sweet Botanicals, 800-931-7530,
gourmetsweetbotanicals.com.

White Chocolate Whipped Cream
Yield: 4 cups | Preparation: 10 minutes

2 cups heavy whipping cream
1 (3.3-ounce) package white chocolate
  instant pudding

• In a large bowl, combine cream and pudding mix. Beat at medium-high speed with an electric mixer until stiff peaks form.
• Use immediately.

Desert Dove Tea Room & Café
for the love of george

Sharon Tuttle has known three important Georges in her life—her grandfather, George; her husband, George; and her best friend, Georgia. "My love for my grandfather, my husband, and my friend has been passed down through cups of tea," says the owner of the Desert Dove Tea Room & Café. "I had to offer that love to the fourth George in my life: St. George, Utah!"

Sharon and her husband retired from California to St. George, a small town in the southwest corner of Utah. Shortly after they finished building a home there, he had a massive stroke in 1999. Sharon promised his doctors that George would show them how well he could heal, and she devoted five years to his recovery, caring for him 24/7. She decided to open a tearoom as a creative outlet for herself and to help George with his recovery. "I opened the Desert Dove Tea Room and Café in 2004 as a way for us to engage with the community and to share our love over cups of tea," she says. "Walking, talking, and smiling, George helps with the tearoom and café."

Although many people in Utah, where 60 percent of the population belongs to the Church of Jesus Christ of Latter-day Saints, do not drink tea, Sharon doesn't see that as an obstacle. "To me, tea isn't about the drink. It's about caring for yourself and others through the peace of a teacup," she says. "By using herbal and rooibos infusions, I can offer this love and comfort to people who avoid caffeine, whether it be for health or religious reasons. Through this tearoom, reaching out to neighbors, swapping stories, everyone can come to share love."

Black Forest Cake in a Glass

Yield: 24 servings | Preparation: 35 minutes
Bake: 18 to 20 minutes | Cool: 30 minutes
Refrigerate: 1 hour

1 (16.5-ounce) package devil's food cake mix
3 large eggs
½ cup vegetable oil
1 cup whole buttermilk
1 cup sour cream
1 teaspoon Chinese five-spice powder
1 recipe White Chocolate Whipped Cream
    (recipe opposite)
3 (21-ounce) cans cherry pie filling
Garnish: chopped walnuts, maraschino cherries,
    and fresh mint leaves

• Preheat oven to 350°.
• Line 2 (12-well) muffin pans with paper liners. Set aside.
• Sift cake mix into a medium bowl. Set aside.
• In a large bowl, combine eggs, oil, buttermilk, sour cream, and Chinese five-spice powder, whisking well. Add cake mix, stirring until well combined. Fill wells of prepared muffin pans three-quarters full.
• Bake until a wooden pick inserted in the centers comes out clean, 18 to 20 minutes. Let cool in pans for 10 minutes. Transfer cupcakes to wire racks, and let cool completely.
• Cut cupcakes in half horizontally, and place bottom halves in 24 stemmed glasses.
• Place White Chocolate Whipped Cream in a pastry bag fitted with a large open-star tip (Wilton #1M). Pipe whipped cream on top of cupcake halves in glasses. Spoon cherry pie filling on top of cream, and pipe more whipped cream on top. Add top halves of cupcakes to glasses. Top with more whipped cream.
• Garnish each with walnuts, a cherry, and mint, if desired. Refrigerate for 1 hour before serving.

Basil & Jasmine Strawberry Shortcakes

Yield: 14 shortcakes | Preparation: 45 minutes
Bake: 18 to 20 minutes

2 cups thinly sliced fresh strawberries
1 recipe Jasmine Simple Syrup (recipe follows)
2 cups all-purpose flour*
⅓ cup sugar
2 teaspoons baking powder
½ teaspoon salt
4 tablespoons cold salted butter, cut into pieces
¼ cup chopped fresh basil
½ cup plus 2 tablespoons cold heavy whipping cream,
   divided
½ teaspoon vanilla extract
1 recipe Vanilla Whipped Cream (recipe follows)
Garnish: 14 fresh strawberry halves

• Preheat oven to 350°.
• Line a rimmed baking sheet with parchment paper.
Set aside.
• In a large bowl, combine strawberries and Jasmine
Simple Syrup. Let stand for 30 minutes to infuse flavor
into strawberries.
• In a large bowl, combine flour, sugar, baking powder,
and salt, whisking well. Using a pastry blender, cut
butter into flour mixture until mixture resembles coarse
crumbs. Add basil, stirring to combine. Set aside.
• In a liquid measuring cup, combine ½ cup cream and
vanilla extract, stirring to blend. Add to flour mixture,
stirring to combine. (If dough seems dry, add more
cream, 1 tablespoon at a time, until dough is uniformly
moist.) Working gently, bring mixture together with
hands until a dough forms.
• Turn out dough onto a lightly floured surface, and
knead gently 4 to 5 times. Using a rolling pin, roll dough
to a ½-inch thickness. Using a 2-inch scalloped-edge
round cutter, cut 14 circles from dough. Place 2 inches
apart on prepared pan. Brush tops with remaining
2 tablespoons cream.
• Bake until edges of shortcakes are golden brown and
a wooden pick inserted in the centers comes out clean,
18 to 20 minutes. Let cool slightly.
• Place Vanilla Whipped Cream in a piping bag fitted
with a large open-star tip (Wilton #1). Set aside.
• Using a serrated knife, cut shortcakes in half horizontally. Pour a small amount of Jasmine Simple Syrup
(from strawberries) onto bottom halves of shortcakes.
Evenly divide strawberry slices among bottom halves
of shortcakes, layering and stacking as necessary.
Pipe a dollop of whipped cream onto strawberries.
Cover with top halves of shortcakes, cut sides down.

• Pipe a decorative swirl of whipped cream on top of
shortcakes.
• Garnish each with a strawberry half. Serve immediately.

**We recommend using a soft winter wheat flour such
as White Lily.*

Kitchen Tip: *Don't assemble shortcakes too far in
advance, or they will become soggy.*

Jasmine Simple Syrup

Yield: 2 cups | Preparation: 10 minutes

2 cups water
½ cup sugar
3 bags jasmine green tea

• In a small saucepan, bring water and sugar just to a
boil; remove from heat. Add tea bags, and let steep
for 5 minutes. Remove and discard tea bags. Let syrup
cool completely.

Make-Ahead Tip: *Jasmine Simple Syrup can be made
ahead and refrigerated in a covered container for up to
2 days.*

Vanilla Whipped Cream

Yield: 3 cups | Preparation: 5 minutes

1½ cups cold heavy whipping cream
¼ cup confectioners' sugar
½ teaspoon vanilla extract

• In a medium mixing bowl, combine cream, confectioners' sugar, and vanilla extract. Beat at high speed
with an electric mixer until stiff peaks form.
• Use immediately.

Make-Ahead Tip: *Vanilla Whipped Cream can be made
earlier in the day and stored in a covered container in the
refrigerator until needed.*

" *Sweets to
the sweet.* "

— William Shakespeare, *Hamlet*

Caramel Cream Puffs

Yield: 24 cream puffs | Preparation: 35 minutes
Bake: 20 minutes | Cool: 30 minutes

¾ cup water
6 tablespoons salted butter, cut into pieces
2 teaspoons sugar
¼ teaspoon salt
¾ cup all-purpose flour
3 large eggs, at room temperature
1 (8-ounce) container mascarpone cheese
½ cup dulce de leche*
Garnish: confectioners' sugar

• Preheat oven to 400°.
• Line 2 rimmed baking sheets with silicone baking mats or parchment paper. Set aside.
• In a medium saucepan, combine water, butter, sugar, and salt. Cook over medium heat until butter melts. Add flour all at once, stirring vigorously with a wooden spoon. Cook, and stir until dough pulls away from sides of pan, 1 to 2 minutes. Remove pan from heat, and let stand for 2 minutes, stirring a few times to cool dough.
• Add eggs, one at a time, stirring constantly and vigorously with a wooden spoon until each egg is well incorporated. (Dough should be smooth and shiny.) Transfer dough to a piping bag fitted with a large round tip (Ateco #809). Pipe dough onto prepared baking sheet in 1½-inch mounds, spacing 1 inch apart. Pat dough peaks down with a damp finger.
• Bake until golden brown, approximately 20 minutes. Transfer baking sheet to a wire rack. Using a skewer or the tip of a pointed knife, poke a small hole in side of each cream puff to allow steam to escape. Let cool completely.
• In a medium bowl, combine mascarpone and dulce de leche, stirring until smooth and creamy. Transfer mixture to a piping bag fitted with a large open-star tip (Wilton #1M). Set aside.
• Using a serrated knife, cut each cream puff in half horizontally. Pipe caramel mixture in a decorative swirl onto bottom halves of cream puffs. Top with remaining halves.
• Garnish with a sifting of confectioners' sugar, if desired.
• Serve immediately.

Make-Ahead Tip: *Cream puffs can be made a week in advance and frozen (unfilled) in heavy-duty resealable plastic bags. Let thaw completely before filling.*

**Dulce de leche is a caramel spread available in the canned milk section of most grocery stores.*

Blackberry-Buttermilk Sherbet

Yield: 9 (⅓-cup) servings | Preparation: 15 minutes
Freeze: 20 to 25 minutes

1 (10-ounce) jar seedless blackberry preserves,
    such as Dickinson's*
2 cups cold whole buttermilk
1 vanilla bean, split lengthwise, seeds scraped
    and reserved
¼ teaspoon ground black pepper
⅛ teaspoon salt
Garnish: edible flowers†

• In a medium bowl, whisk preserves until loosened and smooth. Add buttermilk, reserved vanilla bean seeds, pepper, and salt, stirring to combine. Pour mixture into a 1½-quart countertop ice-cream maker. Freeze according to manufacturer's directions. (This should take approximately 25 minutes.)
• Transfer sherbet to an airtight container, cover surface with plastic wrap, and freeze until ready to serve.
• Garnish individual servings with edible flowers, if desired.

Kitchen Tip: *Ground black pepper may seem to be an unusual ingredient for ice cream, but it provides a counterpoint to the sweetness of the sherbet.*

**It's important to use high-quality blackberry preserves to create a fresh blackberry taste.*

†*We used edible flowers from Gourmet Sweet Botanicals, 800-931-7530, gourmetsweetbotanicals.com.*

The Pink House
where friends and family connect

What would you do if you purchased a tearoom that had been in business for 25 years in a circa-1900 house that had been painted pink? If you loved tea and you loved pink as much as Margo Stewart of Claremore, Oklahoma, does, you would paint the interior walls different shades of pink as well.

"I *am* passionate about tea," says Margo, a California native who moved to Oklahoma more than 40 years ago. (Over the years, her voice has acquired a touch of Southern drawl.) "When I bought The Pink House in 2007, I knew that a tearoom that was just a tearoom couldn't survive here in Oklahoma." That's why The Pink House, in the heart of downtown Claremore (approximately 30 miles northeast of Tulsa), also serves lunch Monday through Saturday from 11 a.m. to 2 p.m. "You can have a pot of tea anytime," Margo points out. The Pink House offers a choice of 55 varieties of tea with two traditional cream scones. But for high tea, Margo insists, you must make a reservation.

"I would like to think that the tearoom serves a purpose in the community—to bring people together," she says. "Our mission statement is The Pink House, where friends and family connect." She has converted quite a few people in Claremore to drinking tea. And not just women, Margo points out. "It's amazing the number of men who come in The Pink House because they really like tea."

Butterscotch-Praline Layer Dessert

Yield: 24 servings | Preparation: 40 minutes
Bake: 10 to 15 minutes | Refrigerate: 6 hours

1⅓ cups salted butter, softened
2⅔ cups all-purpose flour
1⅓ cups chopped pecans, divided
1 cup salted butter, melted
1½ cups firmly packed light brown sugar
2 (3.5-ounce) packages cook-and-serve butterscotch pudding
1 (3-ounce) package vanilla instant pudding
5 cups whole milk
2 recipes Sweetened Whipped Cream (recipe on page 52)
Garnish: caramel sundae syrup, such as Hershey's

• Preheat oven to 350°.
• In a medium bowl, combine softened butter, flour, and ⅓ cup pecans, stirring to blend. Press mixture into the bottom of a 13-x-9-inch baking pan, pressing firmly to create a level base.
• Bake until lightly browned, 10 to 15 minutes. Let cool completely.
• In another bowl, combine melted butter, brown sugar, and remaining 1 cup pecans, stirring to blend. Spread over cooled crust in baking pan. Set aside.
• In a large saucepan, combine pudding mixes and milk, stirring to blend. Cook, stirring frequently over medium heat, until pudding thickens. Pour over pecan layer, and refrigerate until set, 4 to 6 hours.
• Spread Sweetened Whipped Cream over pudding layer.
• Garnish individual servings with a drizzle of caramel syrup, if desired.

Chocolate Truffle Cones with Jasmine Whipped Cream

Yield: 6 servings | *Preparation: 30 minutes*
Refrigerate: 8 hours or overnight

1½ cups heavy whipping cream, divided
2 bags jasmine green tea
2 tablespoons confectioners' sugar
¾ cup semisweet chocolate morsels
6 waffle cones
½ cup fresh blueberries
½ cup fresh raspberries
Garnish: Wilton sugar pearls, nonpareils,
  pearlized jimmies, luster flakes

• In a small saucepan, heat 1 cup cream until very hot but not boiling. (Bubbles should appear around the edges of pan.) Remove from heat, and add tea bags. Let steep for 10 minutes; remove and discard tea bags. Refrigerate infused cream in a covered container until very cold, 8 hours or overnight.
• In a large bowl, combine cold infused cream and confectioners' sugar. Beat at high speed with an electric mixer until stiff peaks form. Cover, and refrigerate until serving time.
• In a small saucepan, heat remaining ½ cup cream until very hot but not boiling. Remove from heat, and add chocolate morsels, stirring until chocolate melts and mixture is smooth. Pour melted chocolate into a

heatproof bowl. Set bowl in a bowl of crushed ice to cool, stirring occasionally. When chocolate is the consistency of cake frosting, place in a resealable plastic bag with a corner snipped off to make a ½-inch opening. Set aside.

• Place waffle cones on a cutting board, and using a sharp serrated knife, carefully cut off and discard approximately 2 inches of cone top, leaving a 4-inch length of cone.

• Divide blueberries and raspberries among waffle cones. Pipe chocolate mixture over fruit to fill cones. At this point, cones can be placed in a covered container and refrigerated for up to 2 hours before serving.

• Just before serving, transfer jasmine whipped cream to a piping bag fitted with a large open-star tip (Wilton #1M). Pipe a decorative rosette onto tops of cones.

• Garnish with sugar pearls, nonpareils, jimmies, and luster flakes, if desired.

Kitchen Tip: To make waffle cones easier to fill and refrigerate, stand each one up in a small juice glass.

Coconut–Vanilla Bean Panna Cottas
Yield: 6 (½-cup) servings | Preparation: 20 minutes
Cook: 3 minutes | Refrigerate: 4 hours

3 tablespoons water
1 (.25-ounce) envelope unflavored gelatin
1 cup heavy whipping cream
1 (13.5-ounce) can coconut milk, such as Goya
½ cup confectioners' sugar
¼ teaspoon salt
1 vanilla bean, split lengthwise, seeds scraped
  and reserved
¼ teaspoon coconut extract
Garnish: fresh edible flowers*

• Place 6 teacups or 6 (½-cup) ramekins on a rimmed baking sheet. Set aside.

• Place water in a small bowl. Sprinkle gelatin over water, and let stand for 10 minutes.

• In a medium saucepan, combine cream, coconut milk, confectioners' sugar, salt, and reserved vanilla-bean seeds, whisking well. Cook over medium-high heat until very hot but not boiling. Remove from heat, and add gelatin mixture, whisking until incorporated. Add coconut extract. Let mixture cool slightly so that it will not shatter delicate teacups.

• Divide cream mixture evenly among teacups, whisking frequently so vanilla-bean seeds do not settle at bottom.

• Cover with plastic wrap, not letting plastic wrap touch surface of cream mixture. Refrigerate until set, approximately 4 hours.

• Garnish each serving with fresh edible flowers, if desired.

Kitchen Tip: Transfer cream mixture to a liquid measuring cup with a pouring spout to make it easier to pour into teacups.

Make-Ahead Tip: Panna cottas can be made a day in advance. Cover teacups with plastic wrap, but don't let wrap touch surface of panna cottas.

*We used edible flowers from Gourmet Sweet Botanicals, 800-931-7530, gourmetsweetbotanicals.com.

GLUTEN FREE

Make-Ahead Tip: *Meringues can be made several days in advance and stored at room temperature in an airtight container.*

Kitchen Tip: *Anchor parchment sheets to baking pans by piping small dots of meringue mixture at corners before placing parchment sheet on pan. This will keep paper in place while piping meringues. Pipe meringue onto parchment paper, pulling tip up to form a drop shape.*

*Make sure pecans are chopped finely enough to pass through a piping tip.

Pecan Kisses

Yield: approximately 32 pieces | Preparation: 20 minutes
Bake: 1 hour | Dry: overnight

3 large egg whites, at room temperature
¼ teaspoon cream of tartar
½ cup sugar
¼ cup confectioners' sugar
1 teaspoon vanilla extract
⅛ teaspoon salt
⅓ cup finely chopped toasted pecans*

• Preheat oven to 250°.
• Line several rimmed baking pans with parchment paper. Set aside.
• In a large mixing bowl, combine egg whites and cream of tartar. Beat at high speed with an electric mixer until soft peaks begin to form. Add sugars, vanilla extract, and salt, beating until incorporated. Continue to beat at high speed until stiff peaks form and meringue is shiny, approximately 3 minutes. Reduce mixer speed to low, and add chopped pecans, beating until incorporated.
• Transfer mixture to a piping bag fitted with a very large open-star tip (Ateco #848). Pipe drops onto prepared baking pans.
• Bake for 1 hour. Turn oven off, and let sit overnight in oven with door closed. (This will help meringues dry out and form a lightly airy texture.) The next day, store at room temperature in an airtight container.

Dark Chocolate–Pistachio Toffee

Yield: approximately 30 pieces | Preparation: 15 minutes
Cook: 8 minutes | Refrigerate: 30 minutes

½ cup plus 2 tablespoons salted butter, divided
¾ cup finely chopped roasted and salted pistachios, divided
1 cup sugar
¼ cup water
¾ cup bittersweet chocolate morsels, such as Ghirardelli

• Line a baking sheet with a silicone baking mat. Spread 1 tablespoon butter in a 9-inch circle on baking mat. Sprinkle ½ cup pistachios over butter circle in an even layer. Set aside.
• Coat the inner top 2 inches of a large microwave-safe bowl with 1 tablespoon butter. Place remaining ½ cup butter in bowl. Add sugar and water. Do not stir.
• Microwave on High until mixture turns very light brown, 6 to 8 minutes. (Because microwaves vary, additional time may be required.)
• Immediately pour hot mixture over pistachios, covering nuts in an even layer. (If necessary, spread mixture with a spatula, working very quickly. Sugar mixture sets quickly.)
• Immediately sprinkle chocolate morsels over sugar mixture in an even layer. Let sit for 1 minute to melt. Spread evenly, using an offset spatula.
• Sprinkle remaining ¼ cup pistachios over melted chocolate.
• Refrigerate until candy is firm, approximately 30 minutes.
• When firm, cut into pieces, using a long, sharp knife and pressing down.
• Store at room temperature for up to 3 days.

GLUTEN
FREE

The St. James Tearoom
celebrating everything british

I f you looked up the definition of *Anglophile* in Webster's Dictionary, you would probably find a photo of Mary Alice Higbie next to the listing. Mary Alice, known to her friends as M. A. (or Emmai as she spells it), has loved all things British—literature, history, and especially the British custom of taking tea—since she was a girl growing up in Albuquerque, New Mexico. In December 1999, she fulfilled a lifelong dream when she opened The St. James Tearoom there.

The exterior of the tearoom looks very New Mexican with its stucco walls, but Emmai has transformed the interior into a series of British vignettes for taking tea, as well as a gift shop that looks like an English marketplace. "We serve a full British afternoon tea," explains Miss Cris, the tearoom's manager. "It's a three-course meal, all finger food, served on a three-tiered tray. Each course is paired with a different tea." The St. James staff chooses the tea pairings, but guests are free to substitute their own favorites from among the 52 teas on the menu.

The tearoom is divided into 17 seating areas, small nooks, and parlors separated by curtains. Each section is named for one of the St. James's "greats"—17 people, ranging from Jane Austen to Winston Churchill, who have made significant contributions to British history.

Cris, who started at the St. James as a server in 2001, says the tearoom provides something most restaurants don't. "We encourage community and relationships." She says that during the two hours of your reservation, "you can get away from everything in your life that is busy and hurried and just spend time with your loved ones over a cup of tea."

Emmai's Cherry-Champagne Sorbet
Yield: 12 (½-cup) servings | Preparation: 30 minutes

2 cups sugar (If using sweetened pie cherries, use ½ cup less.)
1½ cups white grape juice
6 cups frozen, unsweetened tart pie cherries
2 cups champagne
2 tablespoons fresh lemon juice
Garnish: edible flowers*

• In a medium saucepan, combine sugar and grape juice to make a simple syrup. Cook, and stir over medium heat just until sugar dissolves, 3 to 5 minutes. Remove from heat, and let cool.
• In the work bowl of a food processor, combine cherries, champagne, and lemon juice. Process until smooth. Add cherry mixture to sugar mixture, stirring to blend.
• Freeze in a countertop ice-cream maker, according to manufacturer's directions. Transfer sorbet to a covered container, and freeze overnight.
• Garnish individual servings with edible flowers, if desired.

We used edible flowers from Gourmet Sweet Botanicals, 800-931-7530, gourmetsweetbotanicals.com.

GLUTEN FREE

Brown Sugar–Cashew Fudge

Yield: approximately 49 pieces | *Preparation: 20 minutes*
Cook: 5 minutes | *Cool: 2 hours*

⅔ cup evaporated milk
2 cups firmly packed light brown sugar
¾ cup salted butter, cut into chunks
⅛ teaspoon salt
1 teaspoon vanilla extract
1¾ cups confectioners' sugar
1 (7-ounce) jar marshmallow crème
1 cup finely chopped roasted, salted cashews

• Line an 8-inch square pan with heavy-duty aluminum foil. Spray foil with nonstick cooking spray. Set aside.
• In a heavy medium saucepan, combine milk, brown sugar, butter, and salt. Bring to a boil over medium-high heat, stirring constantly. Reduce heat to medium, and cook for 5 minutes, stirring frequently. Remove pan from heat, and add vanilla extract.
• Using an electric mixer, gradually add confectioners' sugar, beating until smooth and creamy. Add marshmallow crème, stirring quickly and vigorously with a wooden spoon until incorporated. Add cashews, stirring to combine.
• Spread mixture into prepared pan, smoothing to create an even layer. Let stand for several hours until fudge is firm enough to cut.
• Lift fudge from pan, using foil as handles, and place on a cutting surface. Using a long, sharp knife, press downward to create clean cuts.
• Store fudge in an airtight container at room temperature.

"There is nothing better than a friend, unless it is a friend with chocolate."

— Linda Grayson

Chocolate Semifreddo with Raspberry Sauce

Yield: 12 (1-ounce) servings | Preparation: 25 minutes Freeze: 4 hours

6 ounces bittersweet chocolate, such as Ghirardelli, finely chopped
2 large eggs, separated, at room temperature
½ cup cold heavy whipping cream
¼ cup sugar
1 recipe Raspberry Sauce (recipe follows)
Garnish: fresh raspberries and fresh mint

• Place chocolate in a medium microwave-safe bowl. Melt chocolate on low in a microwave oven in 30-second intervals, stirring after each interval, until chocolate is smooth. Set aside to cool.
• In a medium mixing bowl, beat egg whites at high speed with an electric mixer until stiff peaks form. Set aside.
• In another mixing bowl, beat cream at high speed until soft peaks form. Set aside.
• In a large mixing bowl, combine sugar and egg yolks. Beat at high speed until pale. Add melted chocolate, and beat until incorporated. (Mixture should be grainy and thick.)
• Add beaten egg whites to chocolate mixture in 3 portions, continuing to beat at high speed until mixture becomes smooth, 2 to 3 minutes.
• Gently fold whipped cream into chocolate mixture until incorporated.
• Divide mixture evenly among 12 (1-ounce) wells of a silicone mold.
• Freeze for at least 4 hours. (Cover with plastic wrap if freezing for longer than 4 hours.)
• Unmold semifreddo onto individual serving plates. Serve immediately with Raspberry Sauce.
• Garnish with raspberries and mint, if desired.

Note: *This dessert contains raw eggs. According to the USDA, people with health problems, the very young, the elderly, and pregnant women should avoid eating foods with raw eggs.*

We used Silikomart's SF109/C (12-well) silicone mini brioche mold (amazon.com).

GLUTEN FREE

Raspberry Sauce

Yield: ½ cup | Preparation: 30 minutes Cook: 5 minutes | Cool: 30 minutes

1 (12-ounce) package frozen raspberries
¼ cup orange juice
¼ cup plus 1 teaspoon water, divided
¼ cup sugar
1 teaspoon cornstarch

• Line a fine-mesh sieve with cheesecloth. Set aside.
• In a small saucepan, combine raspberries, orange juice, ¼ cup water, and sugar. Bring to a boil over medium heat. Reduce heat to medium-low, and simmer for 5 minutes.
• Strain raspberry mixture into a small saucepan through prepared sieve, pressing on solids to extract juice. Bring juice to a simmer.
• In a small bowl, combine cornstarch and remaining 1 teaspoon water to make a paste. Add to simmering juice, whisking until cornstarch mixture is incorporated and juice thickens into a sauce.
• Let sauce cool to room temperature. Use immediately, or transfer sauce to a covered container, and refrigerate until needed.*

It may be necessary to thin cold sauce with hot water, ¼ teaspoon at a time, to achieve desired consistency.

The English Rose
a place for making memories

It's rare that your life dream coincides with someone else's and that when you are ready to lay down the burden of sustaining it, someone is there to lift it up. But that is exactly what happened when Sharon Gilley purchased The English Rose from Angela Becksvoort three years ago. Angela, a native of the British colony of Rhodesia who had established the tearoom in 1997, was ready to retire. Fortunately, she found Sharon who had always wanted to own a tearoom.

The English Rose, in downtown Chattanooga, specializes in the British style of tea, a perfect fit for Sharon. "I had a British friend years ago who taught me how to drink a proper cup of tea," she recalls. "We developed a friendship over tea." Then, a chance conversation with Angela turned into an opportunity to make Sharon's dream come true. It wasn't difficult to say yes.

"The English Rose is a tearoom, but we have a strong lunch crowd," Sharon points out. A British-style lunch is served—including cottage pie, bangers and mash, and steak and mushroom pie topped with a flaky pastry.

Part of the joy of owning The English Rose is hearing all the customers' stories. "With 17 years of history, we have people who came here as children for their first tea experience, and now they are having baby showers," Sharon says. "People tell me how meaningful the tearoom has been in their lives. It's a joy and privilege to be a part of something that makes that kind of memories."

Eton's Chaos
Yield: 8 (½-cup) servings | Preparation: 20 minutes

1½ cups heavy whipping cream
4 (2-inch) Meringues, made the day before, coarsely broken (recipe follows)
1½ cups fresh strawberries, coarsely chopped
Garnish: whole strawberries

• In a chilled mixing bowl, beat cream at high speed with an electric mixer until stiff peaks form, 2 to 3 minutes. (Be careful not to overbeat, or cream will turn into butter.) Cover and refrigerate.
• Just before serving, lightly fold in 4 coarsely broken meringues and strawberries until just covered. Divide mixture evenly among 8 (½-cup) serving dishes.
• Garnish each serving with a whole strawberry, if desired.

Meringues
Yield: 24 meringues | Preparation: 15 minutes
Bake: 4 hours | Dry: overnight

1½ cups sugar
¾ teaspoon cream of tartar
6 large egg whites, at room temperature

• Preheat oven to 200°.
• Line a rimmed baking sheet with parchment paper. Set aside.
• In a medium bowl, combine sugar and cream of tartar, whisking well. Set aside.
• In a clean, dry glass bowl, beat egg whites at high speed with an electric mixer until foamy and doubled in size, approximately 1 minute. Add sugar mixture to egg whites a few tablespoons at a time, beating until combined. Beat until stiff peaks form.
• Using ¼-cup scoop, drop meringues onto prepared baking sheet, approximately 1 inch apart. (Meringues should be approximately 2 inches in diameter.)
• Bake until meringues are crisp all the way through, approximately 4 to 5 hours, depending on humidity. Check for crispness. If meringues are not yet crisp, continue to bake for 30 to 45 minutes. Turn off oven, and leave meringues in oven to cool and finish drying out.
• Store at room temperature in an airtight container or a resealable plastic bag until needed. Meringues will keep for 2 weeks if stored in an airtight container after each use.

GLUTEN
FREE

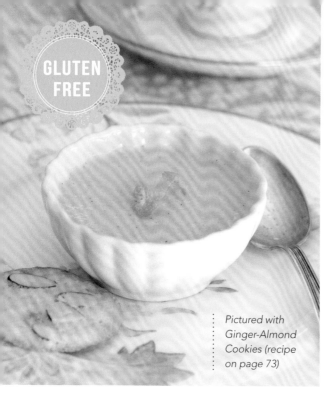

GLUTEN FREE

Pictured with Ginger-Almond Cookies (recipe on page 73)

Vanilla-Rooibos Pots de Crème

Yield: 12 (2-ounce) servings | Preparation: 30 minutes
Bake: 35 to 40 minutes | Refrigerate: 4 hours

2 cups heavy whipping cream, divided
1 vanilla bean, split lengthwise, scraped and seeds reserved
2 tablespoons Rishi Jamaica Red Rooibos blend*
6 large egg yolks
½ cup sugar
⅛ teaspoon salt

• Preheat oven to 325°.
• Place a clean dish towel in the bottom of a baking dish large enough to accommodate 12 (2-ounce) ovenproof ramekins. Set aside.
• In a small bowl, combine 1 cup cream with reserved vanilla seeds. Set aside.
• In a small saucepan, heat remaining 1 cup cream over medium heat until very hot but not boiling. (Bubbles should appear around edges of pan, and mixture should produce steam.) Place rooibos blend in a small heatproof bowl, and pour hot cream over it. Let steep for 10 minutes.
• Strain rooibos-infused cream through a fine-mesh sieve into vanilla-infused cream, stirring well. Set aside.
• In a medium bowl, combine egg yolks and sugar, whisking well. Add cream mixture, whisking until combined. Strain again through a fine-mesh sieve.
• Evenly divide mixture among 12 (2-ounce) ramekins. Place ramekins in prepared baking dish. Fill baking dish with enough water to come halfway up sides of ramekins, being careful not to get water in ramekins.
• Bake until center is set, 35 to 40 minutes.
• Carefully remove ramekins from hot water. Cover, and refrigerate until cold, at least 4 hours. Serve cold.

*Available at rishi-tea.com and at some Whole Foods Markets.

Kiwi, Mango & Coconut Pavlovas

Yield: 10 pavlovas | Preparation: 45 minutes
Bake: 1 hour | Cool: 2 hours

2 large egg whites, at room temperature
¼ teaspoon cream of tartar
⅛ teaspoon salt
½ cup sugar
2 ounces cream cheese, softened
¼ cup sour cream
¼ cup firmly packed light brown sugar
¼ teaspoon vanilla extract
2⅓ cups sliced kiwi
⅔ cup diced mango
¼ cup toasted coconut

• Preheat oven to 250°.
• Line a baking sheet with parchment paper. Using a 3-inch round cutter and a pencil, trace 10 circles, 2 inches apart, onto parchment. Turn parchment over so pencil marks are face down on baking sheet. Set aside.
• In a medium mixing bowl, combine egg whites, cream of tartar, and salt. Beat at high speed with an electric mixer until soft peaks form. Add sugar gradually while beating until stiff peaks form. (Meringue mixture will look glossy.) Transfer mixture to a piping bag fitted with a medium open-star tip (Wilton #21).
• Starting in the middle of each traced circle, pipe concentric circles of meringue mixture outward until circle is filled. Pipe 1 to 2 extra layers on perimeters of rounds to form a rim around the edge of each circle.*
• Bake for 1 hour. Turn off oven, and let sit in oven for at least 2 hours or overnight. (This will help meringues continue to dry and form a crispy shell.)
• In a small bowl, combine cream cheese, sour cream, brown sugar, and vanilla extract, beating at medium speed with an electric mixer until mixture is smooth and creamy. Cover, and refrigerate until ready to use.
• Divide cream cheese mixture evenly among meringue shells. Arrange kiwi slices in shells, overlapping and curving to form a flower shape. Place diced mango in center of each, and sprinkle with toasted coconut.
• Serve immediately.

GLUTEN
FREE

*HOW-TO
on page 128

RECIPE
on page 73

How-tos

Let these step-by-step photos serve as your visual guide while you create these impressive and delicious teatime treats.

GREEK EASTER COOKIES

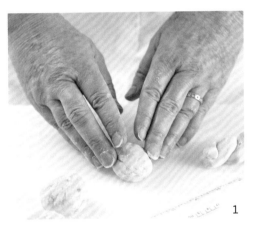

Divide dough into 1½-tablespoon portions.

On a lightly floured surface, roll portions of dough to 6-x-½-inch ropes.

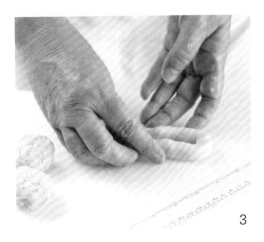

Fold each dough rope in half.

Twist rope to form a braid.

PEACH-GINGER TARTLETS

1

Using a paring knife, cut peach halves into ¼-inch slices.

Arrange longest slices around outer edges of tartlets, overlapping ends.

2

3

Add more slices to make a flower shape.

4

Brush tartlets with reserved heavy syrup.

PAVLOVAS

1. Line a baking sheet with parchment paper. Trace 2-inch circles onto parchment. Flip parchment over.

2. Working from the center outward, pipe concentric circles of meringue mixture until circle is filled.

3. Pipe 1 to 2 extra layers onto perimeters of rounds to form a rim around the edge of each circle.

4. Repeat piping procedure to fill all traced circles. Bake according to recipe.

1

2

3

4

STRAWBERRY ROSETTES

1. Using a pairing knife, make 2 intersecting cuts in each strawberry, keeping the base intact.

2. On each quarter of the strawberry, make a small cut, angling the knife slightly inward.

1

2

TARTLET CRUST

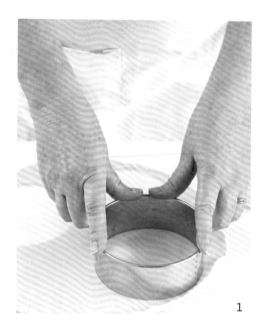

Using a cutter, cut shapes from dough.

1

Press dough shapes into tartlet pans.

2

Trim excess dough.

3

Using the wide end of a chopstick, push dough into indentations of pan.

4

RECIPE
on page 67

ALMOND-APPLE TEA BREAD
(recipe on page 16)

Acknowledgments

COVER

Photography by Kamin H. Williams
Haviland *Louveciennes* teapot and bread and
butter plate*. Herend *Princess Victoria* cup and
saucer[†]. Tiered stand from Maryland China
Company, 800-638-3880, *marylandchina.com*.

CAKES & CUPCAKES

Page 15: Anna Weatherley *Bouquet of Flowers*
platter and Garnier-Thiebaut napkin[†].
Page 18: Christian Dior *Tabriz* bread and
butter plate*. **Page 20:** Mariposa silver cake
stand[†]. Classic lace napkins from Sur La
Table, 800-243-0852, *surlatable.com*.
Page 21: Emile Henry rectangular platter,
302-326-4800, *emilehenryusa.com*. Royal
Winton *Summertime* cup and saucer, dinner
plate, and salad plate*. **Page 23:** Haviland
Galaxy bread and butter plate, teapot, and
cup and saucer*. **Page 28:** Royal Doulton
Dinnerware *1815* rectangular tray from
Macy's, 800-289-6229, *macys.com*.
Page 30: Raynaud *Allee Royale* dessert plate,
cup and saucer, and teapot from DeVine
Corporation, 732-751-0500, *devinecorp.net*.
Page 31: Doily cake stand from Pier 1,
800-245-4595, pier1.com. Fitz and Floyd
Renaissance Peach cup and saucer*.
Page 33: Juliska *Berry and Thread* cake stand;
Anna Weatherley *Anna's Palette* dessert plate[†].
Page 35: Herend *Windsor Garden* cup and
saucer and bread and butter plate, 800-643-
7363, *herendusa.com*. **Page 36:** Petite Treat
mini pedestals from Rosanna, 877-343-3779,
rosannainc.com. **Page 38:** Royal Crown Derby
Posie bread and butter plate, cup and saucer,
and teapot*. **Page 39:** Johnson Brothers *Blue
Willow* cup and saucer*. **Page 42:** Lenox *Rose*
bread and butter plate and cup and saucer*.
Page 43: Bordallo Pinheiro *Rabbit* serving
platter and cup and saucer*. **Page 44:** Lenox
Kate Spade New York *Bissell Cove* accent
luncheon plate*. **Page 45:** Lenox *Rose* cup
and saucer*.

TARTS & CHEESECAKES

Page 49: White scalloped cake plate from
Pier 1, 800-245-4595, *pier1.com*. Bernardaud
Eden Turquoise cup and saucer*. **Page 50:**
Herend *Princess Victoria* rectangular tray[†].
Page 51: Herend *Chinese Bouquet* cup and

saucer; Herend *Chinese Bouquet Garland* dessert
plate[†]. **Page 52:** Coastline Imports *Pink Vine*
cup and saucer from Stash Tea, 800-800-
8327, *stashtea.com*. **Page 53:** Herend *Chinese
Bouquet* dessert plate and cup and saucer[†].
Page 55: Olympia 3 Tier Glass Cake Plate
Stand Server from Amazon, *amazon.com*.
Page 57: Wedgwood *Crown Sapphire* bread
and butter plate and footed cup and saucer*.
Page 59: Anna Weatherley *Anna's Palette*
dessert plate and cup and saucer[†].
Page 60: Olympia 3 Tier Glass Cake Plate
Stand Server from Amazon, *amazon.com*.
Haviland *Louveciennes* cup and saucer*.
Page 61: Emile Henry rectangular platter,
302-326-4800, *emilehenryusa.com*.
Page 63: Christian Dior *Tabriz* bread and
butter plate*. **Page 66:** Annieglass appetizer
tray[†]. **Page 68:** Annieglass appetizer tray[†].

COOKIES & BARS

Page 71: Appetizer platter from World
Market, 877-967-5362, *worldmarket.com*.
Page 73: Juliska *Berry and Thread* ice-cream
compote[†]. **Page 74:** *Tapestry Ocean* dinner
napkin from Hen House Linens.
Page 75: *Tapestry Ocean* dinner napkin from
Hen House Linens. **Page 78:** Wedgwood
Juliet bread and butter plate, cup and saucer,
and teapot*. **Page 80:** Raynaud *Allee Royale*
cup and saucer from DeVine Corporation,
732-751-0500, *devinecorp.net*. **Page 82:**
Annieglass *Ruffle* tray[†]. **Page 83:** Glass
pedestal stands and domes from Pottery
Barn, 888-779-5176, *potterybarn.com*.
Page 86: Emile Henry rectangular platter,
302-326-4800, *emilehenryusa.com*.
Page 87: Lace chambray napkin from Pier 1,
800-245-4595, *pier1.com*. **Page 89:** Fitz &
Floyd *Renaissance Peach* cup and saucer*.
Page 90: Wedgwood Crown *Sapphire* footed
cup and saucer*. **Page 92:** *Incanto White
Lace* small rectangular platter from Vietri,
919-245-4180, *vietri.com*. **Page 94:** Annieglass
serving tray[†]. Lenox *Rose* cup and saucer*.
Page 95: Julia Knight rectangular tray with
handles, 800-388-1878, *juliaknightcollection.com*.
Wedgwood *Wild Strawberry* cup and saucer*.
Page 98: Wedgwood *Sterling* salad plate and
dinner plate*. Key lime quilted place mat from
Pinecone Hill, 877-586-4771, *pineconehill.com*.

OTHER SWEETS

Page 101: Anna Weatherley *Bouquet* of
Flowers tea set[†]. **Page 103:** Schumann
Chateau Dresden cup and saucer*.
Page 104: Fitz and Floyd *Renaissance Mint
Green* dessert plate and cup and saucer*.
Page 105: Lenox *Rose* bread and butter
plate, cup and saucer, and teapot*.
Page 108: Royal Copenhagen *Blue Fluted*
cup and saucer*. **Page 109:** Herend *Princess
Victoria* platter[†]. **Page 110:** Rosenthal
Continental *Ancient Beauty* dessert plate*.
Page 112: Chas Field Haviland *CHF130*
bread and butter plate and cup and saucer*.
Page 113: Cake pedestal from Rosanna,
877-343-3779, *rosannainc.com*.
Page 114: Chas Field Haviland *CHF130*
cup and Rosenthal Continental *Ancient Beauty*
cup*. **Page 116:** Haviland *Silver Anniversary*
plates*. **Page 120:** Raynaud *Allee Royale*
dessert plate from DeVine Corporation, 732-
751-0500, *devinecorp.net*. **Page 122:** Fitz and
Floyd *Renaissance Mint Green* saucer*.
Page 123: Marchesa by Lenox *Spring Lark*
dessert plate and cup and saucer*. **Page 124:**
Royal Doulton Dinnerware *1815* plate from
Macy's, 800-800-289-6229 *macys.com*.

* *from Replacements, Ltd., 800-REPLACE,*
replacements.com.
[†] *from Bromberg's, 205-871-3276,*
brombergs.com.

Editor's Note: *Items not listed are from private
collections. No pattern or manufacturer information
is available.*

SPECIALTY TEA PURVEYORS

*The teas recommended in the Tea-Pairing Guide on
page 11 are available from one or more of these fine
companies.*
Capital Teas, 888-484-8327, *capitalteas.com*
Elmwood Inn Fine Teas, 800-765-2139,
elmwoodinn.com
Grace Tea Company, 978-635-9500,
gracetea.com
Harney & Sons, 888-427-6398, *harney.com*
Simpson & Vail, 800-282-8327, *svtea.com*
Tealuxe, 888-832-5893, *tealuxe.com*
Teas Etc, 800-832-1126, *teasetc.com*

Recipe Index

Editor's Note: Recipes listed in pink
are gluten-free, provided gluten-free
versions of processed ingredients
(such as flours and extracts) are used.

TEAROOM DIRECTORY

"Everywhere people have known it, tea has always been one of the arts of civilized living..."

—James Norwood Pratt,
James Norwood Pratt's Tea Dictionary